JUST BEFORE DARK

Stories from a land of lost content

Perry Leary

Copyright © Perry Leary 2024

This book is sold subject to the condition that it shall not, by way of trade or otherwise, be lent, resold, hired out, or otherwise circulated without the publisher's prior consent in any form of binding or cover other than that in which it is published and without a similar condition including this condition being imposed on the subsequent publisher.

The moral right of Perry Leary has been asserted.

ISBN-13: 9798329340686

To everyone who did their best, especially Patricia Leary.

ACKNOWLEDGEMENTS

My thanks are due to those who lived these stories with me or recounted them to me.

I thank many family members for their advice and encouragement, including Andrew, Stephanie, Vanessa, James, Bridget, Tim and Helen Leary and my brother Mick. Friends who have kept me active and out of trouble and who have flattered my efforts with praise include Peta, Pat, Norman, Peter and Kevin from South Africa, Vivien, John and Ewen in England, Mary, Colin, Carol and many others in Ireland, Mo, Adrienne and Marie in the Americas and Judith in Jerusalem.

Hilaire Belloc summed up the trials of this life best when he wrote

There's nothing worth the wear of winning, but laughter and the love of friends

Special thanks to Yanina Goldenberg of KINDLE BOOK PUBLISHING for expert help in publishing my stories.

CONTENTS

PREFACE 1
FIRST STEPS 4
LIGHTFOOT LADS 9
LOUIS AND THE SECRET TINS 14
THE SCHOOLBOYS 22
ONCE UPON A TIME 29
SUCCESS TOUCHES SOME 34
TEACHERS 42
BOYS AND GIRLS COME OUT TO PLAY 50
UNIVERSITY 57
MEDICAL SCHOOL 64
THE CASUALTY DEPARTMENT 70
CONSULTANTS 79
THE GARDEN OF EDEN 85
THE BOERS 93
DURBAN MEDICAL SCHOOL. SPOOKS. 103
THE MEDICAL COUNCIL 110
THE THRUST COMPANY 118
AMADODA, ABAFAZI. 124
NEIGHBOURS 132
REGINAH SHANGE 139
EMERSON AND OBED 145
UNSUNG AFFECTION 149
BROOKHOUSE 158
WHITE KNIGHTS 163

PREFACE

The African stories in this memoir have been collected from two earlier books; *Pardonable Offences* and *Happy Highways*. Slight changes have been made to the original texts here and there and the illustrations are, with some exceptions, entirely new. Most are photographs taken during the spring of 2024 in the fantasy world of my garden near Lismore in Ireland. They have been chosen to remind the reader that innocence and beauty survive in those things that I believe have been created purely for our delight.

The motive for presenting these tales in a single volume was simply to provide a record of a way of life that has now all but vanished from South Africa and will, in due course, be the subject of many distorted narratives. During the period in question, roughly 1945 to 1994, no one born in that country, whatever their race, had any notion of what it might be like to live without some form of racial segregation. The life-styles, world views and national histories of "Europeans" and black Africans were poles apart.

In the 1950s Father Trevor Huddlestone, an innocent of the British left-wing, wrote a judgemental book about South Africa entitled *Naught For Your Comfort*. His work attacked government policy and brought into focus the price it was exacting in human suffering. The book's title came from lines in G.K. Chesterton's Ballad of the White Horse:

> *I tell you naught for your comfort,*
> *Yea, naught for your desire,*
> *Save that the sky grows darker yet…..*

The good father made a very strong case against apartheid although he slightly overstated his case. He could not have foreseen that the unsympathetic autocrats of the old white National Party would, in due course, be replaced by men of darkness, by rampant materialism and the dictatorship of an incompetent and uncaring black government. Fortunately, neither white nor black nationalism has so far succeeded in crushing the human spirit entirely. One must suspect, however, that such an outcome is foremost in the future plans of Marxists or religious fanatics of one stripe or another.

The title of this book has been chosen because the stories are taken from a time just before the period of darkness and economic collapse that has accompanied the government of South Africa by the African National Congress. City dwellers in that country might well point out that the darkness is also literal for some of the day since the regular supply of electricity has proven beyond the expertise of the "comrades" appointed to maintain infrastructure.

Of course this volume might just as well be entitled **Unjust** Before Dark, given the unfairness of the apartheid years. Puns aside, the murderous criminality, corruption and lack of accountability of the present century make for a nostalgic view of the old South Africa when one looks into the dying embers of what was once an imperfect country but one of significance and worth. Throughout this book a degree of circumspection has been used in that the real names of many individuals are not used, even though most of them have long since perished. There are exceptions however; notably those of Reginah Shange, the African war heroes, a few politicians and the unfortunate, unsung Brookhouse amongst others.

It is my hope that some of the decency, good humour and compassion of the ordinary individuals in these tales from the past will be obvious and that readers might take the witness of these uncelebrated people to heart. May the day come when we all learn, black and white, Gentiles and Jews, to love our neighbours as ourselves.

Perry Leary

Ballinadine, 2024

FIRST STEPS

The war years from early 1940 to late 1945 were spent with my mother, granny and older brother in a quiet corner of what was once the Cape Colony but was then part of the Union of South Africa. Grahamstown, the cathedral town in which we lived, was in the area developed and farmed by the British 1820 Settlers and where my paternal great-grandfather, an Irishman from County Kildare, had lived from his arrival, as a boy drummer with the 75th Regiment of Foot, in about 1838 until his death in 1896.

As a very small boy our modest suburban home seemed palatial to me but it was no more than a standard bungalow of the times, set in a garden perhaps 25 paces long and 15 wide. The roof, painted red or green at different times, was of corrugated iron and this surface magnified the beautiful sound made by falling rain, particularly at night when people were at home and the streets were still. Rainwater was collected from the roof by a simple system of strategically placed gutters that drained into large storage tanks behind the building. This was mainly used for irrigating the garden but, once collected and stored, provided a useful reserve in case of drought or supply problems from the local government reservoir. Each room had at least one large sash window that could be left open quite safely to help circulate any cool breeze on a hot summer's day. Climatic extremes were not that much of a bother and were usually accepted with stoicism.

There was no shortage of fresh air and if anyone glued themselves to the cathedral door in protest against pollution caused by the Dean's Austin 7 we never heard of it.

Whether or not the mid-1940s were a just, peaceful and humane period in the history of race relations and of South Africa in particular might be worth debating. What is factually so is that in 2023 the homes around number 19 Milner Street, Makhanda (as Grahamstown has become) boast electrically operated steel gates, high walls topped by razor wire and, in a few cases, security cameras. Breaking and entering became a growth industry around the year 2000 and, as I write, there are some 100 murders and 150 rapes every day of the week in that country which currently hosts a population roughly the same size as that of Great Britain.

Eighty years ago, most of the descendants of settlers from the British islands were monarchists who thought of themselves as "English". In fact, they were considered so by their Afrikaans and Black compatriots whether they were essentially Irish, Scots, Welsh or indeed English from either the north or south of that country. The absurdity of living in Africa whilst professing loyalty to a German king on an English throne and fighting in a world war that would kill millions of people of many nations and all races was lost upon almost everyone. Each performance at public cinemas (or bioscopes, as South Africans called "movie-houses" then) closed to the strains of the strange, slightly camp, British National Anthem played whilst a picture of nice king George Vl, with his country's flag fluttering behind him, was projected on the screen. We were expected to stand respectfully to attention during what would have been an entirely farcical ceremony were it not for the existence of Adolf Hitler and his psychopathic friends.

Information technology was still years from development and so life was simple and secure in Grahamstown. Children knew nothing of the terror their contemporaries in Europe faced. Britain, according to the parents and grandparents of that generation, was without doubt the greatest country on earth, the source of everything that was good and noble and was destined to dominate the civilized world forever. A land, so we heard, both of heart's desire and of hope and glory. We knew nothing of the crimes committed by greedy empire-builders, and were taught to honour the virtue, courage and grace in adversity of the ordinary soldiers and farmers whom the Victorian establishment used as their pawns. Typically, the incompetence and failure of the Scott expedition to Antarctica trumped anything Amundsen might have achieved if one took raw courage and determination into account. Propaganda, half-truths and blatant lies flourished long before the age of the internet and its "platforms" dawned.

We played our childish games with our schoolmates and, sometimes, with the children of our Nguni servants, content in the knowledge that we, being of British blood, were somehow ordained by God Himself to be their masters. Of course we were also, according to our own blinkered society, a good cut above the Latins, with their emotional incontinence, and also the coarse rabble inhabiting countries such as the USA and Australia. So the story went anyway.

When he returned home after the war, my father was transferred from the bank where he worked in Grahamstown to a post in Cape Town, some 500 miles away. He was uncomfortable amongst his old colleagues, most of whom had not seen fit to "join up" (as voluntary service was called) and fight against the enemy. It is clear that some men could not be released from their key posts in civilian life but possibly others felt it inconvenient to disrupt their own lives and respond to the aggression of an insane little enemy of civilisation who was reputed to have but a single testicle. Probably idleness, self-interest and old fashioned cowardice influenced many of those who decided to stay at home during the conflict.

There was no family connection with Cape Town and so we moved from the friendly and comfortable surroundings of a relatively small town to live amongst strangers in the suburbs of a major city.

For the first few months we lived in what was termed "a residential hotel", run by a ferocious landlady with mercilessly dyed pitch-black hair, much mascara about the eyes, scarlet lipstick and a large, short-tempered dog that kept watch at the front door. In truth, the "Devonshire Hills", was more of a boarding-house than a hotel but perhaps it had pretensions. The difference could be easily determined by the absence, in the case of a proper hotel, of any porridge and/or boiled cabbage smell on crossing the threshold of the building.

Places were found for me and my brother at an excellent and well-established school within walking distance of Devonshire Hills. We were left to find our own new friends.

After a few months in these surroundings we moved to a rented bungalow in a pleasant suburban setting in Abbotsleigh, just off Sandown Road, Rondebosch. Typical of the time and place, without post-codes, the name of the house was engraved and painted on a board at the front gate. There was more than a little irony to the fact that, like the Devonshire Hills hotel, "Ambleside" was named after a place some 8000 miles away in England, where it rained almost daily and life was tough by comparison with sunny South Africa. There was a lawn large enough for games of tip-and-run cricket and in the back garden a couple of tall pines offered a climbing test for my brother who would one day distinguish himself in epic mountain rescues. The front garden was separated from the quiet road by a splendid hedge of orange-flowered Cape honeysuckle within which peculiar-looking, well-camouflaged chameleons could be found, hunting for flies or other tasty insects.

A modest enough property, Ambleside was surrounded by rather more impressive buildings, including a private maternity hospital and the expensive homes of a tea and coffee magnate, a dentist, an ophthalmologist, and an ear nose and throat surgeon. Today the simple house in which we lived until 1953 no longer has a flowering hedge. In common with its neighbours and the old family home in Grahamstown-Makhanda, it is surrounded by a high wall with some six strands of electrified, barbed wire running across its top edge. There are notices near the electronically-controlled entrance gate advising that the property is protected by an armed-response team. One might gain the impression that intruders would not be welcome in suburban homes that once were left unlocked and open for most of the day.

The back garden and the tall pine-trees are gone, replaced by an even smaller house that has been shoe-horned into the space that was cleared for it. All part of the brave new African world that has disappointed nearly everyone other than those most closely connected to the corrupt politicians that have come to power following decolonisation.

LIGHTFOOT LADS

One day, soon after the move to Cape Town, I happened to be near the front gate of my new school some five or ten minutes before the first morning lessons were due to begin. There I witnessed a sight that I have remembered ever since and have described in detail elsewhere. It was the almost ceremonial arrival at school of Louis the Russian.

Louis was a little, curly-headed, slightly bat-eared, son of Jewish, immigrants who ran an old-fashioned grocery store at Rondebosch Fountain, then part of the village about 3 miles beyond the junior school.

Each week day, just before the first morning bell, a bicycle bearing human cargo passed the local "Indian" corner shop (A.M. Banderker and Sons), at the end of the road. Attached to its handlebars, was a wicker basket, perhaps 2 feet by 2 feet square and 18 inches deep, in which loads of assorted groceries were normally carried for delivery to homes in and about the suburb.

Little Louis, aged about seven at the time, would arrive at the gates loaded into the front basket, like a cauliflower or pocket of oranges. His legs would be hanging over the front, stockings near his ankles and school cap not quite correctly aligned. His arrival was comical to behold and always delighted those pupils who were loafing about near the school entrance.

Louis the Russian always appeared on time, "delivered" by the Tembu "boy" who would help his little passenger down, hand him his school bag (containing chicken-fat sandwiches and books) and ride away after bidding him goodbye. He came back to take Louis home at the end of the day. I was to become great friends with the little Russian, God love him.

After a couple of years most of the schoolboys had their own bicycles which were usually second-hand and slightly the worse for wear. Traffic was light in the mid-twentieth century and boys as young as 10 or 11 would ride several miles to school along the main roads, unsupervised and without protective gear of any sort. The strong coastal winds gusted fiercely from time to time and could dislodge a small boy from his saddle but otherwise there were few hazards.

At the preparatory school, boys were naturally just as uncouth and grubby as healthy young lads anywhere else. Once dismissed from lessons and released into the schoolyard, we went out in the sunshine, noisily playing marbles, wrestling, learning to bat and bowl, sidestep and pass inexpertly in games of cricket or slightly chaotic touch-rugby. Another sport, with a brief vogue, involved running past boys regarded as "weeds" or "swots" and ripping open their fly-buttons to no specific end. Probably not a woke attitude particularly since we had no insight into pronouns of choice or indeed any other form of mental illness.

Time soon passed and from the age of about 10 the boys began to put away childish things and to take part in organised sports; rugby, cricket, athletics, gymnastics and boxing. The teachers sorted them into groups by age and size and, as a result, many friends were separated and would only meet in class, where chatter was not allowed, or in the yard during breaks. So it was that Louis and I would usually only get together after the school had closed for the day.

One afternoon, I was riding home on my bicycle when I heard loud laughter and shouts of glee coming from the direction of two boys of about my own age, perhaps between 10 and 12, standing under an oak tree in Sandown road. One boy was animated and athletic-looking, the other, his elder brother as it turned out, seemed quieter, almost solemn, and wore wire-rimmed spectacles; a studious-looking boy. They were entertaining themselves by heaving acorns and small rocks at cars passing by down the hill and then hiding themselves from sight behind the tree. When I came nearer they stopped their game, which had scored no direct hits as far as I could tell, and spoke to me in halting, heavily-accented English.

The boys were named Georges and Michel and explained they had come from Belguim, with their parents and grandmother, as refugees. Of course this was as exotic to me, in my ignorance of Europe, as hearing that they had landed the previous evening from the planet Mongo or that they were the nephews of Rockfist Rogan or Bulldog Drummond. They seemed anxious to talk and make friends, consulting each other in French when at a loss for an English word.

Friendship developed in the months that followed. We all joined the same scout troop and Georges introduced me to a new hobby, collecting small reptiles that we captured on local expeditions to the open fields that were still common amongst the suburbs of Cape Town. These were then kept in makeshift vivaria that we built in our parents' gardens. Mostly we found the harmless little snakes that lived under boulders and discarded sheets of corrugated iron on vacant ground; most snakes were not particularly handsome, even to a small boy's eyes. There was one species, however, that was much sought after and seldom found. It was the beautiful, non-venomous, Aurora Snake, pale green in colour with an orange dorsal stripe down the length of its eighteen-inch body. It was worth any three Russet Garden Snakes in a swop between young ruffians. Hard as it was at the time to part with any of my snakes, I gave Louis the Russian one as a birthday present when he turned 12. Something he reminded me of when I met him at a school reunion 65 years later.

The Belgians attended the same school as I did but we were in different years and so only met after school or during the long summer holidays at scout camps, exploring the open, sunny, veld and swimming in mountain pools. At length we went on to study at different universities and never saw each other again. Georges, who had been naturally studious, calm and hard working at school and had shown great interest in biology, became a professor of physics at a university in the Cape. Michel, the far more excitable and physically active brother, was an outstanding gymnast and athlete who had a successful career in commerce after leaving school and settling in Canada where he raised his family.

Neither of them ever returned to the engaging pastimes of stoning cars or collecting snakes as far as I am aware.

There is much more to tell of Louis the Russian anon. I met my dear boyhood friend at a reunion held at the old school many years after we had completed our studies there. As in 1946, Louis was brought to school in some comfort and style. Not on a delivery-man's bicycle this time. His carer was no longer a Tembu "boy" but a young woman. She stood quietly behind my old friend's wheelchair.

LOUIS AND THE SECRET TINS

During the middle years of the 20th century, most English-speaking white boys enjoyed something akin to a charmed life in South Africa. Certainly that applied to those fortunate enough to live near Cape Town. The sun seemed to shine on the wild ericas, proteas and silver-leaf trees below the mountain almost every day and the sea was warm and welcoming to young and old, segregated by race as a matter of course. Admittedly there were occasional plagues of stinging blue-bottles to cope with but shark-attacks were very rare and at that time few people in government thought that city sewage was best disposed of by drains that flowed directly into the rivers or the sea. If it rained heavily, as it sometimes could in winter, there was always the option of schoolboy rugby played on the muddy fields or, occasionally, a visit to the bioscope, (as the cinema was called), near the homes of my friends Louis the Russian and Joey the Ginger.

Louis lived behind his parents' grocery store, right next door to the only gentleman's barber in town and opposite other small shops, a haberdashery and a bakery. The manager and barber was an extrovert named Jacobus Johannes Viljoen, known to his regular customers as "Oom", the Afrikaans for "Uncle". His general appearance and facial features, in particular, suggested that he had a long-term, serious, interest in the health-giving properties of tobacco and a few of the better Cabernet Sauvignons from nearby vineyards in Paarl and Stellenbosch. A man in his fifties, Oom Viljoen tended to wheeze and cough a lot, occasionally spitting into a large pocket handkerchief with a tartan motif. Beside the barber's chair was a counter upon which he kept brilliantine, razors, clean towels and shaving soap. He would rest his half-smoked cigarettes there between puffs, whilst chatting away to his customers and cutting their hair. The cigarette ash and cut ends of hair were kept from falling onto clothes or down collars by an almost clean white sheet that he draped across their shoulders. The deflected ash and hair ends would accumulate on the floor around his feet. A homely enough spectacle, one might say.

The interior of Mr Viljoen's domain was somewhat carelessly arranged. The entrance, leading to the main barber's workshop, was a space just large enough to accommodate a cash register placed on a low glass cabinet in which items that might catch the eye were displayed. Some of these were set out in neat rows of small tins. Within the working area, which was a room of perhaps 5 by 5 paces, six rather ordinary chairs were arranged along two walls for customers waiting their turn. There was a large mirror opposite the barber's chair together with a washbasin with two fine imitation antique taps and a shelf for a collection of coloured liquids including bay rum, shampoo and other items unfamiliar to small boys. These included dyes for vain men greying at the temples and tapers that the Oom would sometimes light with a Lion brand match and use to singe his customer's hair. This was to help prevent baldness, or so we were told.

Conversations between the barber and his grown-up customers, were fascinating to 11 and 12 year old schoolboys. We would sit in our battered school blazers listening to the men talking whilst pretending to read the dog-eared old comics and glossy two-year-old magazines that were piled on a table near the chairs for those waiting for a "short back and sides" haircut. To judge by what he said between bouts of coughing, Mr Viljoen seemed to have two main interests. When not discussing rugby and the merits of Dennis Fry and Sammy Loots, local rugby heroes, he would be telling all and sundry about the reliability and other splendid qualities of the mysterious tinned goods in the glass display case near the door. They were offered for sale to adults only.

From what was said we learned that each tin cost two shillings and sixpence and contained 3 mysterious items which real men, and especially rugby-players, might need "for the weekend". The barber would refer to them as "preventatives", sometimes throwing in a confusing reference to postal deliveries received from France. What these items might prevent and exactly how the French might be involved we were unable to fathom. Brand names on the tins read Gold Tex, Crepe de Chine, Ramses and, most exotically, Sheik. The Crepe de Chine label stated that the goods were "transparent". Not to us, certainly. Understanding the interesting ambitions of young or even older men who invested in "a tin of 3" was, mercifully, quite beyond us.

Of course we trusted that, in due course, someone would enlighten us as to the content and purpose of the two-and-sixpenny tins. We were not all that impatient to learn the truth and, for the moment, Mr Viljoen's opinions on who would shine at the next inter-university rugby match were of greater interest to us.

If we did not know what to make of the trade in condoms, help was soon at hand for some of us thanks to Louis the Russian and his older brother, Gabriel. A second or third year university student, Gabe, as he was known, had his own room in the family's small apartment behind his parents' grocery store. One afternoon, whilst looking for a spare pair of socks in one of his brother's drawers, Louis discovered a small hoard of Mr Viljoen's preventatives "for the weekend". After relentless, if poorly directed, questioning by his younger brother, Gabe lost patience and did his best to explain their purpose to him. Louis shared this new, inside, knowledge with three of us a day or two later, when we went to his home to play.

Invitations to visit Louis the Russian after school came every three or four weeks and were irresistible to any small boy with a sweet tooth. The apartment was reached through a back door in the shop where his parents remained all day, hard at work. Louis's kindly mother, a short, plump lady in apron and slippers, decorated with multi-coloured pom-poms on their tops, would stop the little procession of friends as they passed by her counters and refrigerators and present each boy with a small bottle of a pink or green fizzy drink. These liquids, an unholy mixture of water, sugar and artificial flavouring were referred to as "minerals" for some reason. They were like nectar to a small boy but were banned by parents in most of our homes in the well-founded belief that they would rot teeth almost overnight. Sometimes Louis' friends would also be presented with a toffee or small chocolate too. All this happened well before the western obesity epidemic. We were very active as youngsters and no doubt simply burned up calories for much of the day. Indeed, I can remember only one boy nicknamed "Fatty" and, by today's standards he was lean as a long-dog.

The entertainment during visits to Louis' home followed a regular pattern. Rowdy little boys would sit together reading Superman and Captain Marvel comics, go into the small courtyard to throw a tennis ball against the wall or argue about the virtues of various local sportsmen. Of all our heroes, the most popular was possibly Donny Mills, a skinny, laconic, baseball pitcher in the local team. He was admired by his small fans for the way he chewed tobacco on the baseball mound and then spat on the ground as a kind of punctuation between each of his pitches. To copy this within sight of a teacher at school would certainly earn a caning and his behaviour was therefore seen as daring and an expression of independence. Whether Donny Mills had any interest in being caned, we never knew.

On the great day of revelation, just when we were becoming restless, Louis announced that he had something interesting to show us in Gabe's bedroom. Not knowing what to expect, we followed him to a large mahogany chest-of-drawers set against one wall by a window. With some ceremony Louis the Russian opened a top drawer in which handkerchiefs and rolled up pairs of woollen socks were neatly arranged and called us to his side. Amongst the socks there rested a small, flat tin of the type so regularly glimpsed in the cabinet by the till in Mr Viljoen's barber shop. Inscribed on its lid were the immortal words *Gold Tex, The Gilt Edge Prophylactic, ¼ Dozen*. At first, there was excitement because we thought that we would at last learn the secret kept by "Oom" Viljoen and his adult customers but then, being well-mannered and obedient boys, we began to worry that our invasion of Gabriel's room might be detected. A banning order that included an end to pink or green fizzy "minerals" would surely follow.

Louis, however, was unconcerned and, with a flourish, took the tin from amongst the socks and opened it to reveal the tightly-packed contents. The mixed emotions of excitement and nervousness gave way to bewilderment. Nestling in the container were three objects that we were quite unable to identify. They were, in fact, brand-new contraceptives, rolled up and each prevented from unravelling prematurely by its own thin paper belt. Louis, now recognized by his friends as an expert, lifted one of the three from the tin and announced to us that "this is a French letter".

I was not convinced. Though I recognised the term Mr Viljoen sometimes used it still remained a mystery. No matter how strange people in France might be (and of course one sometimes heard alarming reports of what they were apt to eat) surely even the men and women of a manifestly perverse nation would write to one another on paper, albeit in French.

To make matters worse, Louis added to our bewilderment, by claiming that these tightly-wrapped "letters" were designed to be unrolled over a man's penis (though that was not the word he used). They would be placed there in the same fashion as the rubber finger-stall used by matron at school to hold a dressing in place on a lacerated thumb or fore-finger. He also gave us the astonishing news that Gabe always wore one of these French letters, for protection, when he "went" with a girl. What!?

Of course we did not know precisely where Gabriel usually "went" with a girl and, being unaware that "went" was used euphemistically at the time, imagined that he fitted himself with one of these mysterious "protectives", whenever he took a girlfriend to a film, the beach, a barbecue or perhaps a rugby match. Acceptable enough perhaps, but exactly to what end, we wondered. Perhaps it was to protect his person from annoyingly bold insects, such as the bees, wasps, horse-flies or even mosquitos that might approach his inheritance via the open ends of his khaki shorts on a warm day. There was also the possibility that a nasty, stinging, blue-bottle could invade his swimming trunks whilst he took a dip in the Indian Ocean near Muizenberg. If either of these were to be avoided, we could see that a properly-applied Gold Tex might be a very useful shield against undesirable consequences. Indeed so.

Of course there was at least one other possibility. What if these exotic devices were simply used as fashion statements of some kind? Grown-up chaps like Gabe, of Russian or other foreign origin, might choose to wear their transparent French letters on special social occasions, in the same way that our own fathers and uncles would don club or regimental ties when they went to church or a business meeting in the city. We rejected that explanation on the grounds that none of Mr Viljoen's clients at the barbershop seemed obviously foreign, though one couldn't really be sure about one or two esteemed members of our high-school band who were sometimes at the shop, fellows named Tzemis, Empedocles and Zoccola.

Children love sharing a secret even when it is one that is beyond their understanding. We wondered, though we did not ask, why Gabe did not simply spray his undercarriage with an insect-repellent or at least find something more appealing with which to decorate himself such as a string of miniature festive (Christmas or, in his case, Hannukah) lights. A small bell such as adorns a pet cat's collar or budgerigar's cage might also provide an interesting distraction during the excitement of field sports. He could then keep the French letters for use in emergencies such as when he suffered an intimate injury and needed to hold a small bandage in place in that sensitive area. Elastoplast can be painful to remove from delicate surfaces.

When next we went for a haircut, we were not really all that much the wiser for looking in Gabriel's drawer. We merely knew that the customers who spent two shillings and sixpence on a tin of three would be going somewhere with a girlfriend. Perhaps they went to the Curzon cinema nearby or even the university swimming-pool where their stylishly dressed private part would presumably be hidden from view by trousers or swimming trunks. Would the girls even know this or indeed care? Would a bouquet of red roses please them more? No one knew.

The barber shop and the grocery store were bought by developers many years ago and demolished overnight. A filling-station stands on the site today. Sadly, no blue wall-plaque commemorates that this spot was once a hub for condom sales in Rondebosch or that here some nondescript but inquisitive small boys once learnt dubious facts about the uses of "French letters" from their friend in the know, Louis the Russian.

THE SCHOOLBOYS

The Rondebosch high school still stands in its original, beautiful setting. The early twentieth century buildings are surrounded by extensive sports-fields and neat gardens. The grounds and nearby suburban area are sheltered by a range of mountains that, on their eastern side, run down to sandy beaches washed by the Atlantic Ocean. The school buildings and adjacent land were developed with the financial support of wealthy past pupils during the fifty years before my friends and I arrived there. Most of us had attended the associated preparatory school together before promotion to senior classes in 1951.

Every boy was taught a wide range of subjects during their first years at high school but the final 2 years involved a degree of academic streaming, with boys roughly divided in accordance with their ability and interests, as perceived by their teachers.

Most of us lived within 3 miles of the place and walked or rode our bicycles to class carrying backpacks that contained homework books, sandwiches and perhaps sports kit and a spare handkerchief. There was also a boarding establishment to accommodate boys from distant towns. Some came from just beyond the mountains that separate the Cape Flats from the vineyards of the Overberg and others from as far afield as South West Africa (Namibia) and countries that were then known as Southern and Northern Rhodesia (now Zimbabwe and Zambia). These boys would travel for 2 or 3 days by train between their homes and the school each term. Unsurprisingly, given the boredom inherent in long rail journeys across an often featureless landscape, boys from the old colonies were amongst the first of my contemporaries to begin exploring the dubious delights of smoking cigarettes, drinking cheap wine and pursuing spotty schoolgirls.

Admissions to the school were diverse to some degree, though not in the sense of that word as it is now commonly used in western society. Only male children were admitted and they were all supposed to be, superficially at least, members of the white race. There were a few boys from old Cape families whose DNA would most certainly have revealed an interesting mix of European, Malay and perhaps Koi or San bloodlines, reflecting the country's history from as far back as the first European settlements in the 17th century. Though teased at times, they were more often envied for the relative ease with which they developed a handsome tan in the Southern African sun. At the time there was ignorance of the connection with malignant skin diseases and so a tan was seen as healthy and manly. The pretty "peaches and cream" complexion of recent immigrants was scornfully referred to as "a London tan" and the mark of a "weed". Man and boy, South Africans were astonished when the touring British Lions rugby team, pink and white all over, gave the sunburned Springbok heroes a very hard time in the first rugby test of 1955. It seemed that balance and decency were restored when the likes of Karl von Vollenhoven and Wilf Rosenberg either outran the pale "English" players or else ploughed them into the turf during the Newlands rugby test later that year.

Louis the Russian was by no means the only "different", and therefore interesting, boy. There were many others, including the ever-ebullient Joey Bercovich, a ginger-haired baseball and Hollywood-film fanatic, who lived in a family-run hotel together with his own small regiment of older brothers.

One boring summer's afternoon, Joey organized a chalk-throwing battle in one of the classrooms. This event, celebrated as "**the** chalk-fight" by small boys for several years thereafter, resulted in the wanton wastage of a 2 month supply of coloured blackboard chalks and a classroom turned into something resembling an art installation at the Tate Modern gallery. Joey could be considered an unconscious forerunner of some of the heroes of 21st century "art". Never in the history of human conflict had so many coloured chalks been sacrificed by so few (Winston S. Churchill, 1952). In any event, participation in the "chalk fight" resulted in a punishment of 6 "cuts" with the headmaster's cane for each of the five young vandals involved.

Joey later became a multimillionaire by virtue of a clever strategy he used to make strong drink, available to all and sundry well before supermarkets began to sell alcohol at discounted prices. Sadly, Joey, the ginger livewire, succumbed to diabetes long before reaching the biblically allocated lifespan of three-score years and ten.

Amongst the rugby players and other young ruffians were boys of a more sensitive nature who suffered from existential angst, knew poems by heart, played musical instruments and supported the debating and dramatic societies. These were the kind of boys described as "weeds" and "swots" by Nigel Molesworth, the great fictional historian of St Custard's School. All the pupils were referred to and spoken of by their surnames, so the need to agonize over the use of preferred pronouns was never an issue. Possibly there was far less mental disease amongst the general population at that time than today.

Each year at least one major play, often an operetta, was presented by the schoolboys, partly out of tradition but also, perhaps, as a discipline. The few talented youngsters who made up the drama group were usually coached by a teacher who was interested in the arts rather than sports and who was, often, "a confirmed bachelor". Rumours were almost invariably put about by kind ladies of a certain age that these gentle souls had experienced tragic disappointments in love and, like characters from a Victorian novel, would suffer quietly and miserably alone until the end of their lives. Mothers of the boys baked cakes for them. Times have changed.

The less said about the woeful nature of most school plays, the better. These productions were regarded as a torture to be endured by some of the loyal relatives and friends who sat on the uncomfortable seats of the school hall, watching whilst the works of Gilbert and Sullivan or Agatha Christie were laid waste. One or two very talented actors did emerge however.

A boy named Nicholas White, was much admired for his beautiful strawberry-blond locks and naturally long eye-lashes and was always in demand to play female roles in school productions. He was certainly well-suited for such parts in a boys' school full of grubby, rugby-mad, sometimes oafish urchins. Of course, nearly 70 years ago, no deranged fantasist suggested reassigning his gender and a small, though very pretty, boy he was mercifully allowed to remain until puberty intervened. In due time, after matriculating, he went to London. There his talent blossomed and Nicholas became a celebrated member of the theatrical community. He broadened his range to include direction, production and theatre management, also becoming a well-respected and prolific playwright. Possibly he was grateful that his first opportunities to appear on a stage had been at school with an audience of thoroughly uncouth young boys. It must have been a great relief for him to appear before informed, appreciative audiences as an adult. Somewhere in the school archives there is a photograph of a beautiful ten-year-old boy, in costume as a geisha with an open fan in hand and suitable headdress above a perfectly combed wig, curtsying before a larger boy dressed as some sort of Eastern potentate. I stand in the background with the extras, including Joey, the boy destined to be make millions from a chain of liquor stores, Geoffrey, a future Professor of English, several rugby-playing "heavies" and Louis the Russian. The older boy who played the emperor was Peter Rutherford, son of a non-conformist priest, who later featured on television in British soap operas and in the occasional "B" film. In spite of our tender years we ruffians looked out of place and slightly embarrassed whereas Nicholas and Peter, gifted as they were, quite clearly did not.

Two of the most interesting boys were the sons of a latter-day hero, a Prussian aristocrat who had opposed Adolf Hitler and his gangsters openly during World War ll and paid for this with his life. The elder boy, Helmuth the Count (as indeed he was) and his brother had somehow escaped from Germany with their mother, who had South African connections. He was solemn, dignified and reserved and the boys, being ignorant of German history and basically an uncultured rabble, were not interested in the tribulations of his immediate family and did not care about his famous and impeccable lineage. Any of our own ancestors who fought at the Somme or in Flanders would have known, and possibly trembled at, the very mention of his great-uncle, a certain General von Moltke.

In some ways Helmuth was an unreconstructed 19th century Prussian. On one occasion, he made an unexpected and heartfelt contribution to a boring school history lesson. Whilst discussing the activities of Napoleon Bonaparte, the teacher (a slightly threadbare English fellow with a recurrent shaving-rash and red-rimmed eyes) observed that France and Prussia had made a habit of waging war against each other at one time. The Count, to whom this was not news and who had been dozing in his desk like a peer in the British House of Lords, raised his head from his slumber. He made the briefest of comments before nodding off again. "Ja! And always we defeated them!" This uttered with what might be described as a certain degree of satisfaction and emphasis upon the word "we". Indeed.

Helmuth, with his astonishing and heroic family story, went on to Oxford and, in due course, became a highly qualified industrial chemist. He worked for a time in a West German industrial area and retired in the end to a quiet and beautiful town in Vermont, USA. This town is just a short drive from the home of the von Trapp family who were made famous by a musical, "The Sound of Music".

Two less aristocratic, but equally memorable, boys were Rhodesians who came down to the Cape to attend the school and spent each term living at Canigou, the school boarding-house.

Ewan C. Greenfield, a boy of impeccable Scottish heritage, was the son of a judge. He had an astonishing ability to spit at and hit a moving target ten or more paces away. In this respect, the accuracy of his expectorations rivaled those of various African, venom-spitting, serpents such as the Ringhals and the Egyptian Cobra but without the same distressing effects. He was blessed with a fine command of the English language and could also perform a fairly convincing imitation of the great satchel-mouth trumpeter Louis Armstrong. Later in life he obviously retired from expectoration becoming, in a show of further versatility, a member of the British school inspectorate (no pun intended).

John Patrick Fletcher, on the other hand, had a quite different talent. The son of a colonial knight and a secret smoker of unfiltered truly foul Rhodesian tobacco from the age of 13, he always had an old-fashioned cigarette-lighter in his pocket or, at least, within easy reach. After the lights were put out at night in the boarding establishment he would sometimes entertain the other young delinquents by ventilating his backside whilst simultaneously igniting his cigarette-lighter. Generally, an impressive column of fire would issue forth from his posterior, which briefly became a sort of organically-based, if not eco-friendly, flame-thrower. This was an astonishing, if coarse and socially unacceptable, form of self-expression that he could be relied upon to repeat more or less on demand.

Years later, during the bush-war in his own country, Lieutenant Fletcher bravely led a platoon of Matabele soldiers in counter-insurgency operations against the ragged but determined followers of Messrs Mugabe and Nkomo. No one ever heard whether or not he had an opportunity to mobilise his unusual skill to the alarm and bewilderment of the enemy; a pity if he did not. As it happened, he passed into history uncelebrated and with no imperishable memorial. In this, he shared the fate of most of humankind.

ONCE UPON A TIME

During my schooldays, no matter what weekday activities might entail, Saturdays and Sundays were our own to spend with our families at home. Sometimes it was then, with time on our hands, that chance meetings taught us more than we might have learnt in the classroom.

South Africa was a racially segregated society at that time and admission to all the high-schools was not only determined by race and gender but also by home language. So white and black, boys and girls and Afrikaners and "the English" were mostly kept apart. At Rondebosch there were a few boys who were Afrikaans speakers at home but whose parents had sent them there to be educated in an "English" school for one reason or another. These were almost invariably amiable, tough, open-hearted boys who were fairly good at all sports but most notably at Rugby football. Some, amongst them, had skills that they had presumably developed out of boredom on some remote farmland as very small boys. One typical fellow, named "Brandy" Pienaar, could never really master the English language but was able to entertain everyone by drop-kicking a rugby ball over the crossbar of the rugby posts in his bare feet from prodigious distances. Yet another, "Suntan" Beukes, a suspiciously brown youngster of about 12, seemingly knew how to handle farm machinery almost from birth and would be allowed to pilot the ungainly school tractor, pulling an old-fashioned golf-course lawnmower over the extensive school sports-fields. Such Homeric feats mesmerised the politely raised, more delicate and less versatile, "English" pupils.

During my childhood and teenage years, I had no interaction with boys of other races beyond an occasional quick nod of the head in the direction of any child who came to the house with the Malay laundryman or who brought messages from the township for our Xhosa housemaid. Then one day, playing by myself kicking a ball about on an open field beside our home, there followed an experience that I have never forgotten and that still brings tears to my eyes.

At the time, our home was situated in a garden suburb perhaps 10 miles from the city centre to which my father would commute each day. Homes were neat and tidy and the streets lined with trees. These were sometimes flowering Australian species but more often they were lofty pines, bent slightly in the direction of the famous Cape south-easterly winds. These firs were the territory of starlings, crows and grey squirrels. Immediately opposite our back gate there was an open field, preserved at the time as a recreation area. The field was partly surrounded by old established trees but there were no shrubs or flower beds at all and the central area, perhaps 30 by 30 yards in extent, was flat and covered with scrubby grass. Quite ideal as a sports field for a small boy who had no idea how favourably his surroundings compared with those of youngsters living in the less appealing areas set aside by the government for those whose skins were not white.

We were by no means a wealthy family but, to mark some occasion or other, my father gave me a rather battered, man-size, leather rugby ball. It might have come from a jumble-sale or perhaps from a friend who was connected to a rugby club. In any event, to a 15-year- old boy who loved the game it was a wonderful present and I would kick it about on the open, grassy field across the road for hours at a time, pretending to be Dennis Fry, Hennie Muller, or some other now forgotten South African rugby hero.

One afternoon, whilst playing about in this way, I noticed a boy of roughly my age who was standing on the pavement at the edge of the field, watching my game with apparent interest. He was neatly dressed in a white shirt and khaki shorts and his slightly curly black hair was shiny and perfectly brushed. Whether he was a Cape Malay or what is now referred to as of "mixed-race" I am unable to say but he was certainly a "coloured" person and would not have been allowed to attend my school, sit beside me in a cinema or travel in the same coach on the trains that ran between the southern suburbs and the city. None of that crossed my mind; here was a possible playmate and I called him over to join me. He hesitated for a moment then, smiling broadly, came onto the field.

Probably we spent no more than an hour together, running, passing the ball back and forth and kicking it to each other. Never mind, Einstein's theory of relativity operated and it seemed like an endless time of pure happiness. No doubt, the angels looked on with approval. Perhaps even they wiped away a tear or two in the end.

My new friend, caught up in the sheer novelty of acceptance by a white boy, suddenly remembered that he was on a mission for his mother and told me that he still had a walk of about 3 miles ahead of him. He stopped playing, handed me the ball and looked into my face intently, as if to commit it to memory. Possibly he was hoping for some memorable, intelligent or encouraging remark from me. Alas! I was very young, ignorant and quite out of my depth. He was not lost for words, however.

"Thank you for **seeing** me on the street and for playing with me," he said in an accent identifiable to any Capetonian. "You are very kind". He walked away but turned back after about 15 paces, looked at me closely again and said "I hope that one day you will be a rugby Springbok". The ultimate best wish. Then he was gone; we never met again.

At school we knew each other by surnames alone, so it did not occur to me to ask my unexpected friend his name or to volunteer mine. Even nameless, he was a real boy and not a hallucination, an atavar or part of some supernatural test. No, in retrospect, what took place was one of those blessed experiences of light and goodness that we have now and then in life's journey. Sadly we are often unable to fully appreciate them at the time and can never return to either the exact time or place.

How stupid, brutal, un-Christian and ultimately futile it was for a national government to, in effect, legislate against friendship between people of different races. Whatever became of that little boy, God love him? Was our game something he still recalled years later? Did that brief experience soften his attitude towards white people when he became an adult and was subjected to all the unfairness and insults that South African society so freely offered? I pray that he was able to live and enjoy a happy and contented life, apartheid and the disastrous, crooked, incompetent and racist African National Congress notwithstanding. Who knows the answers? That meeting, after all, happened once upon a time many years ago.

In truth, "once upon a time, never comes again".

SUCCESS TOUCHES SOME

If a successful political career is synonymous with fame and fortune then the majority of my contemporaries were abject failures. Cynically, it might be claimed that the school did not encourage and nurture the sort of ineptitude, dishonesty and insincerity that are nowadays the hallmarks of many, if not most, elected public representatives. Instead, conceit, lies and narcissism were actively discouraged and what used to be called "a Protestant work ethic" reigned supreme. Incompetence, contempt for the poor and an ability to mislead others were not considered minor personality flaws or even virtues as appears to be the case these days.

Nevertheless, a few youngsters did ultimately dabble in politics or make themselves noticed on its fringes. Probably the least distinguished of them was a boy named, for this narrative, Aubrey Levitt. He was the son of a respected family, whose patriarch had presumably come far south towards the beginning of the 20th century to avoid the persecution of Jews that was then the norm in parts of Europe. As happens amongst a small proportion of asylum-seekers to this day, Aubrey forgot his family's debt to the new country fairly quickly and chose to become involved in attempts to overthrow the state by violent means.

At school he first came to the notice of more senior boys as a friend of Nicholas White, the superb and ultimately successful actor. He was not as gifted as Nicholas although, some years later, a high-court judge did comment that his evidence in a terrorism trial had been a really fine exhibition of theatrical posturing. After leaving school, Aubrey registered as a student at the local university. Even then, as now, such institutions offer impractical courses to those with rather limited talent or imagination and insufficient interest, commitment or potential to enter business or the professions. To them, the university was simply a place where contacts were made and, for those close to the borderline of sanity, provided a platform upon which to parade various (often Marxist) neuroses.

At the time, the South African government followed a policy that had its origins in colonialism but had been brutally refined, extending racial segregation to exclude the majority of the population from many of the benefits that normally flow from a democratic and even-handed system. Opposition to the unseemly policies of the nationalists came from moralists, decent moderate stalwarts and also, naturally enough, unhinged leftists. Such opposition was loud and not without risk; though there was nominal freedom of speech, threats were made routinely by government spokesmen, passports were confiscated and a number of people were incarcerated without trial. A few vocal opponents of the system suffered unfortunate, fatal accidents. Peaceful protests were usually mocked by government supporters or else ignored entirely. Agitation and public demonstrations were not uncommon and were, in general, put down ruthlessly. The authorities of the day were more concerned with maintaining order than extending reasonable rights to all the diverse peoples of the country. That said, the South African regime was no way near as ruthless and autocratic as its main critics, such as the Soviet Union and most African and Arabian countries. It was also far more democratic than some of its friends in, for example, the South American dictatorships.

In this climate there emerged some activists amongst white university students who believed, in their crass immaturity, that nothing positive could be achieved without violence. They began a campaign of bombing state installations and, amongst other foolish actions, solicited the advice of a former British soldier and borderline psychopath on how to plan and conduct a guerrilla war. The romantic but sadly naive Aubrey, by this time a leading light in the left-wing national students union, became an active member of one would-be-terrorist group and was arrested after a railway signal was blown up near his home.

At about the same time as he was arrested, a bomb exploded at a main railway station, fatally wounding an old lady and badly mutilating a child. This provided the security police with an excuse to subject Aubrey to less than gentle treatment which included thoughtfully making sure he understood that he might well be hanged in terms of the anti-terror legislation then in force. Aubrey buckled under interrogation and not only betrayed his friends and co-conspirators but also turned state witness against them in exchange for amnesty. Not cricket. In court, the judge remarked that to call him a rat was to give rats a bad name.

Aubrey, the amateur revolutionary, left the country on an exit visa and settled in England where, after an unhappy period, he became a successful academic, at least in the opinion of people in the muddy and unquiet sea of eccentricity and delusion that is the British liberal left. He was apparently highly regarded in those circles as an authority on human development, an accolade of sorts even if it came from the indifferent university where he worked. After much rending of garments on his part, Aubrey became reconciled with several of the friends he had betrayed and helped send to prison for long spells.

He died of cancer aged 73. His school friends were bewildered by his foolish behaviour and thought that, given his sensitive nature, the political situation and the cruelty with which apartheid was applied had badly affected the balance of his mind. Others chose to draw a line under his quasi-political activities and simply recall the boy; an eager little fellow, lisping and slightly girlish, auditioning for a part in the next school play. That is how I remember him.

On the other hand, Cecil Fothergill, who made no memorable impression on the school in any sphere whatsoever, was a chap who had what it took to enjoy some degree of success as a politician, albeit in Britain. The articulate son of English expatriates, Cecil had all the misplaced self-confidence of that race, so irritating to those who do not quite believe in Britain's all round brilliance and everlasting greatness. After school and a few years at a local university, where he followed one of the aimless courses on offer, he repaired to England. There he enjoyed a brief career in the City before becoming a hard-working but largely invisible member of parliament.

There was to be something of a hiccup in Fothergill's career, however. One Sunday, a newspaper belonging to the less discreet section of the British press reported that Cecil had been a keen participant in what was referred to as "a three-in-a-bed romp". Allegedly he enthusiastically engaged himself in intimate activities with two young women, identified by exciting pseudonyms such as Tracey and Chelsea, in the relative privacy of a London hotel bedroom. He had done what he could to impress them, not just with his manly talents, which were apparently quite up to speed, but also by making insulting comments about the worthlessness of his seniors in the Tory party. Cecil's words, and other sounds, were helpfully recorded on tape by one of the two young women, who happened to be temporarily in the employ of the Sunday newspaper concerned.

The editors were delighted to have this "scoop", of course, but adopted their customary self-righteous position when reporting "Three-in-a-bed-gate". By the tone of what was written, foreign readers might conclude that the overwhelming majority of English people were habitually chaste to the extent of being celibate. Perhaps so, although it might also be argued that Cecil was unusual for a Tory in that he preferred to express his instincts assisted by girls rather than boys. He resigned after this particular scandal but his work ethic was such that he was soon forgiven by the Conservative party (peccadillos of members of parliament and of the rest of the establishment being widespread) and, after a brief interval, returned to the fold. Our man kept his head and, maintaining a dignified silence regarding his personal and domestic habits, emerged to resume progress up the political ladder. His career ended in the House of Lords where he could sit with a great many other dubious citizens of the realm and could appear in the house whenever he felt inclined to drop by to earn an attendance allowance.

Cecil Fothergill MP was fortunate in that all this happened long before public admissions of any enthusiasm for heterosexual self-expression became seen as perverse by members of the "woke" generation, particularly when a "privileged" white man was involved. On the other hand, Cecil's era was also that of the celebrated Cynthia Payne, who was well-known to the great and the good. She kept a productive bawdy house, frequented by otherwise respectable members of the political, legal and clerical elite of both right and left-wing persuasions. So Cecil had played no more than a small part in a somewhat shabby tradition that is still enthusiastically followed to this day.

Two others also made themselves known in spite of spending their schooldays as nonentities. Both were small and nondescript, of slightly above average ability scholastically and undistinguished at any sport more physically demanding than marbles or darts. One, Rupert Lightfoot, became a village solicitor and then entered local politics as an afterthought. With no real aims, ideals or even ideas, he was eventually returned to parliament as a member of the official opposition party. This was a small liberal group that, though brave and vocal, had little or no influence on how the country was governed. Furthermore, no matter what was raised under parliamentary privilege, public pronouncements and protests had to be strictly restrained, to avoid attracting the unpleasant attentions of the sinister national security police. The so-called "Special Branch" had an iron fist without so much as a velvet glove to conceal it. These were cruel and unsettling times.

Rupert carefully considered the facts and very sensibly decided that the safest way forward would be to keep his status as an MP, stay out of trouble and collect his more than adequate parliamentary salary each month. He chose to amuse himself by spending what might, somewhat ironically, be called his down-time with some of the ladies that gather about men they regard as powerful and useful, such as members of parliament and wealthy business executives. Rather similar to the much younger groupies famous for shadowing rich rock-stars, no matter how ugly, diseased or unkempt they might be.

For a man of the same physical stature and appetites as the late dictator Benito Mussolini but without his political power, impressive uniforms, horses or Italian charm, Rupert did very well with the ladies. In those days when Elvis "The Pelvis" Presley was still very much celebrated, he was spoken of as "Enis" by his camp-followers. His nickname did not connect with any particular political agenda.

The other small boy, whose career at school passed almost entirely unnoticed, was named Michael Fleetwood-Jones, or thereabouts. To the general astonishment of his high school classmates, who remembered an ordinary scholar, he enjoyed a successful university career, eventually graduating with a doctorate in zoology from a respectable British institution. In due course, he became an internationally-known author, writing a number of books filled with unsubstantiated observations that had more to do with superstition and magic than with science, reality or truth. They appealed to the public at large and became best sellers.

He was much in demand in certain circles and could, occasionally, be seen pontificating solemnly on television about riveting questions such as whether long-lost rings or watches ultimately find their owners or if root vegetables and cabbages feel pain and have souls. A master of fiction, he invented a mysterious and romantic personal background that greatly added to his image amongst his more gullible readers. This was an approach he first developed at school, where his fictitious claims of noble antecedents or stories of astonishing (and highly improbable) sporting or social adventures during the long summer holidays tended to be ignored by his disrespectful and grubby contemporaries.

Part of his often-repeated narrative was that as a boy he had been almost entirely educated by Kx'a-speaking San hunter-gatherers and, in particular, by a stone-age shaman he met in the Kalahari. This was a brilliant stroke of the imagination though probably borrowed from another somewhat inventive guru, Laurens van der Post, who used to mine some of the same territory. In fact, Michael had certainly never ventured much beyond the city centre throughout his early years and had lived the life of a conventional middle-class youngster. Later, he certainly spent time in less developed parts of the world, prospecting for bizarre material to present in his books. He would have liked to be seen as a character worthy of a Rider Haggard novel and worked hard at achieving such a profile but, in the end, became more like one of the characters in a story by P G Wodehouse.

Though he was never a member of a club called "The Drones", nor mixed with the likes of Bertie Wooster, he began to insist upon always being addressed as "Fleetwood". At school he was known as "Mike" or "Jones", which were a bit commonplace for someone eager to inflate his gravitas, if not his height and physical presence. As he became better known through his writings he would be photographed in a pose, perhaps copied from the portrait of some Edwardian writer or philosopher, with his right elbow on his knee, fist supporting his chin, as he gazed at some paranormal hinterland visible to him alone. Due to his middle-class, colonial background, he lacked the ability, so ingrained in a certain type of native Englishman, to have absolute faith in his own legend or to take himself entirely seriously. So he overlooked the importance of dressing in bedraggled fashion like an Oxbridge eccentric and failed to wear a large medieval signet ring when posing for photographs. If he ever smoked a pipe, wore copper bangles or grew a Zapata moustache is unrecorded.

Whatever Michael's flaws and frailties, he travelled widely, collected wives now and then, made a great deal of money, had a kind heart and was celebrated in various circles inhabited by his gullible and sometimes marginally insane followers. Not a bad legacy after all.

In retrospect, by pretending to be what they undoubtedly were not and acting a part, each of the last two little men added much to the gaiety of other people's lives in one way or another. Possibly their mild, harmless and entertaining charlatanry caused each of them significant inner stress given that both developed derangements of the central nervous system and died at relatively early ages.

In truth, they are both missed.

TEACHERS

Whilst teachers were always addressed by their pupils as "Sir", most of them were spoken of in private by their nicknames. These names usually had their origins in peculiarities that had been noticed by the most observant and least respectful of the schoolboys. A few had no nickname at all and were known to the boys by either their surnames or, in a few cases, their Christian names. The possibility that some eccentricities might have developed as a result of personal tragedies, sorrow or traumatic experiences during the world war that had ended just a few years earlier, never occurred to boys who had yet to develop much by way of either sensitivity or compassion.

Decades later, some "old boys" would still remember the likes of "The Canigou Ghost", a mathematician who, it was rumoured, had survived the dreadful Battle of Delville Wood during the Great War and, having lost his brother in the carnage, never slept again. He would study the stars, sit and meditate or walk slowly and silently about the school boarding hostel each night until dawn. Others were "Budgie", a fine and dedicated teacher with a poorly repaired broken nose and parrot-like quality to his voice and "Freddy the Fidgeter" who, perhaps as a stress reaction, made sudden alarming, in-coordinated and purposeless movements in class. Brian, a history master with bad dandruff, taught that nearly all the leading figures of the past were either clever people with detestable traits or loathsome and untalented fools with no more than a few redeeming features. World War ll was not included in the curriculum yet, so we never learnt what the well-hidden virtues of a Stalin or a Hitler might be. We would emerge from his classes with reservations about any number of historical figures, from Wellington and Napoleon to Cecil John Rhodes and Paul Kruger. Brian's robust opinions were mostly justified, of course.

Perhaps the most popular members of the teaching staff, at least amongst the boys were "Dudley", a gentle, kind, slightly effeminate, man who had returned from World War ll bewildered and afraid and Jack, an eternally cheerful wood and metalwork master. Purely on the basis of his smooth skin and counter-tenor voice, the latter master was supposed to share an unfortunate deficiency with the recently deceased German chancellor, a Mr. Hitler. Since we were both coarse and callow, most of us knew the wartime song that celebrated this alleged deficit in the trouser department.

"The Octopus" was primarily a geography and geology master but also responsible for religious studies and sex education. He was, like Jacob's brother Esau, an hairy man of impressive physique and what seemed to be potent masculinity. His perpetually stern visage had an almost demonic quality because of his piercing gaze and thick, dark, overhanging eyebrows. Ocky, as he was usually called out of earshot, appeared to be a lover of nature with, perhaps, a liking for naturism. He would end geology excursions to rock formations on some remote stretch of the Cape coast by inviting his pupils to join him in a bout of nude surfing.

This would be followed by 15 minutes of, uninhibited, touch rugby on the beach, no doubt a measure intended to remedy the physical effects of bathing in the icy Atlantic Ocean that washes the west side of the Cape. His apologists would probably have described his behaviour as "muscular Christianity" but the possibilities of voyeurism and exhibitionism, (he being, in more than one sense, a big man), come to mind. A keen lay-preacher, he was later appointed headmaster at another boys' high-school where his prowess with the cane became legendary. One suspects he was a man who might have made an interesting study in clinical psychology or, these days, become the subject of an investigation by one fringe group or another.

Friday afternoons in summer were set aside for school cadet parades. Several teachers morphed into army officers and would appear in smart uniforms to direct proceedings; a noble sight. Whether any of them simply enjoyed role playing and would have preferred to change into women's lingerie and high heels, one cannot say. Who knows how society would have reacted then had such harmless, (though now all but compulsory), behaviour come to light?

All the boys began their *faux* military service as privates in one of the 10 or 12 platoons that made up the three companies of the school "regiment". Keen pupils could be promoted to the ranks of sergeant, company sergeant-major and lieutenant, particularly if they showed an interest in military matters and attended at least one training camp during a summer holiday period. Boy-officers wore peaked caps but rank-and-file cadets, to the great annoyance of war veterans, were issued with soft, khaki, caps indistinguishable from those worn by Rommel's Afrika Korps whom South Africans *inter alia* had fought in the Western Desert.

No doubt the nationalist government, a few of whose members had been outspoken apologists for the Third Reich, were trying to make an unsubtle point. In the early 1950s most of the established South African regiments still took pride in including the British crown in their insignia and jingoism was alive and well, especially in Natal and the Eastern Cape. This was an understandable state of affairs less than 10 years after a world war.

About once a term the cadets would be issued with Lee-Enfield rifles of Anglo-Boer war (1900) vintage and marched through the suburbs for an hour or two, led by the school band playing stirring marching tunes just slightly off-key. The old rifles were stored securely in an armoury beside the main rugby field; all had been rendered useless long before but spectators along the streets were not to know this. As it was, the antique weapons lay heavily and uncomfortably on the shoulders of reluctant teenagers, who would have preferred to be swimming or playing cricket. Whether the purpose of these "route marches" was to keep the boys honest or to intimidate persons of other races, I cannot say.

Cadet parades only took place during the dry months of the year.

Most of the masters who participated held the honorary rank of captain in the country's army reserve although one, Mr. Tuesday, known to the boys as "Rubberguts", had been promoted to the rank of major and so wore crowns on each of his shoulders. These were later replaced by a badge that was less offensive to the republican-minded Afrikaner government.

The major, a doppelganger for Captain Mainwaring of "Dad's Army" fame, was a plump, physically unimposing and unintentionally pompous little man. Commanding officer or not, it is unlikely that he would have struck fear into the heart of Nazi storm-troopers or, for that matter, an Italian wine-steward or an average lady's hairdresser. He did, however, have sterling qualities. These included dignity, presence and the fact that he was a highly educated, civilized and well-informed individual.

Major Tuesday, when not on parade, also happened to be a first rate teacher of Latin, English and the scriptures and it is for these gifts that he is most gratefully remembered.

When called upon to take a class in scripture or English Mr. Tuesday tended to concentrate upon best-loved quotations taken from the Bible or a book of poems prescribed for young pupils. The poems that Rubberguts Tuesday returned to time and again tended to be classics set in the distant past and of the sabre-rattling variety. It is true that many boys first heard the wicked phrase *"Dulci et decorum est, pro patria mori"*, from him in person, though it is uncertain whether he subscribed to that disgraceful old lie himself. Lord Byron's Destruction of Sennacherib and Macauley's poem, Horatius at the Bridge, stirred the blood of impressionable boys with rising testosterone levels:

And how can man die better
Than facing fearful odds
For the ashes of his fathers
And the temples of his gods.

Perhaps Rubberguts really did believe in the Latin adage quoted above. It seems more likely that he simply loved the cadences of poetry though, if questioned, he might have claimed a preference for sudden death in battle over a longer life ending in helplessness and senile dementia.

In scripture lessons, he was particularly fond of quoting the prophet Isaiah:

All we like sheep have gone astray

To small boys, of our age, this was a bewildering statement. We were well aware of certain infringements that would earn a caning at school but could not quite understand where woolly, moronic, sheep might come to grief. Not, one presumed, by breaking windows, swearing, self-abuse or smoking cheap cigarettes behind the bicycle shed with Johnny Hainsworth and "Froggy" Roberts. Later, no doubt, we all took our chances and fell within the scope of Isaiah's words.

Once or twice each year, until 1954, Mr Louw, an ex-teacher of perhaps 70, would come to the school as a stop-gap for someone on vacation. He tended to teach mathematics and arithmetic to the junior years. At each lesson, he would set the class a number of sums to solve and go off to the lavatories for 20 minutes to smoke one of his foul, unfiltered, Senior Service cigarettes. Nothing if not a good sport, Japie Louw, would signal his imminent return to lessons by coughing loudly and stamping his feet on the concrete floor of the passage leading to the classroom door as he approached.

Once back in class, he would go from desk to desk looking carefully at the efforts of each pupil. In the top pocket of his suit, (navy-blue with pin-stripe, Stuttafords sale, January 1946, £15) he always carried 4 or 5 pencils. These were wooden, usually HB, and yellow or red with a small pink eraser at one end. If annoyed by the stupidity of some unfortunate boy, he would brandish one of these pencils and hammer the blunt rubber end a few times against the head of his victim. This was always accompanied by a brief rant, informing his victim, in fine rural Afrikaans, that he was a "snot-headed idiot with termites for brains". Not entirely correct from the scientific point of view and probably not sentiments regularly expressed in the halls of Eton, Harrow, Rugby or Winchester one imagines. Nevertheless, this was an accurate enough assessment of some of our number. Japie seldom drew blood or left visible bruising.

In spite of his tendency to use the rubber end of his pencil as a weapon of maths instruction, Mr. Louw's lessons were enjoyed by most of us in the junior years. This was because he had once coached the school first-fifteen and still had a phenomenal memory for rugby minutiae. He would spend the last ten minutes of each lesson writing the names of every Springbok rugby player from the 1910s to the 1930s on the blackboard. He had the full attention of almost everyone in class as he spoke of his heroes and told us about the exploits of legendary players such as Benny Osler, Danie Craven and Louis Babrow. Homeric stuff to small boys. Accordingly, few, if any, grudges were ever held against him.

Japie died under the wheels of a suburban train perhaps 8 years later. Whether by choice or not, no one knew.

All of the teachers appeared to be in favour of the strict disciplinary regimen of the 1940s and 1950s. The measures applied were quite severe at times and would doubtless now be seen as nasty and cruel, even nightmarish, by most child psychologists. Probably they would have a point in that, looking back with 20:20 vision, it is clear that a few of the teachers had a rather poorly hidden sadistic streak.

The least original form of punishment was naturally enough a caning administered by the school principal or one of the more senior teachers. There were, however, some slightly more inventive ways of keeping young, unwashed, rebels in order. Talking in class would usually attract the non-corporal imposition of what was known as "lines". The culprit would be made to write down the following sentence 100 times in neat, copperplate, script:

I must not be intoxicated by the lugubriousness of my very own verbosity

Notwithstanding their limitations and human defects, most of the teachers did, at least in my view, a worthwhile job of turning a young rabble into decent, useful human beings.

BOYS AND GIRLS COME OUT TO PLAY

Attitudes were mostly sensible and conservative in Cape Town of the 1950s although it would be straining the truth to suggest that the young were uniformly refined and obedient, in spite of the best efforts of their parents and teachers. Almost nothing was known of so-called progressive thinking and there was scant propaganda from the more absurd extremes of American "culture", given the absence of television and the internet. The films of various British and American icons provided images of bravery, goodness and decency to impressionable young fellows, irrespective of what might be happening in reality behind the scenes.

Science still insisted that there were only two genders. Being either male or female at birth and forever thereafter was accepted as a simple biological fact, based on one of two chance couplings of X and Y chromosomes. So, astonishing or even shocking as it might be to dysfunctional modern generation Z, boys actually knew they were boys and, from the age of about 15 or 16, looked forward to wicked adventures involving some of the pubescent girls down the road at the Girls High School.

Before the internet came into being, average twelve-year-olds were very unlikely to be exposed to pornography. Occasionally an older boy, probably of European origin, would gather a few friends around him in the playground and show them a grainy, dog-eared ancient sepia photograph that he had found when rummaging amongst old discarded papers at home. These works of art were known to us as "French Postcards". Of course, in those days, anything deemed unseemly such as condoms, venereal diseases or even being idle at work was likely to be blamed upon the French, Spanish or Italians. Roughly speaking, the equation was C (continental) = A (abomination). This was an absurd and ignorant conceit, of course.

The interpretation of "dirty postcards" was, happily, way beyond most of us. Faded photographs usually depicted an undressed couple in an old-fashioned setting featuring floral wallpaper, and a great many curtains and other drapery, replete with fringes and bows. The models tended to be buxom women and their partners slightly pale skinny little men with splendid moustaches and doleful expressions. Evidently, whatever else might be involved, the protagonists seldom gave the impression of enjoying themselves. Often the shrimp-like men would be naked but for a pair of inelegant, striped socks (sometimes with a toe protruding). These Romeos seldom resembled any of the leading men cinematic of the day and it was difficult for us to work out precisely what their interest was in their stocky lady-friends. In one case, the male "model" was completely naked but for an oversized Homberg hat that rested upon his ears, pushing them outwards as if they were bat's wings. We had to concede, after discussions at the age of 11 or 12, that some adult amusements were obscure. The entire point of these "postcards" was lost upon us.

If there was great ignorance amongst the pre-pubertal boys of that time, we were filled with healthy curiosity all the same. Just a year or two later an age of enlightenment dawned as we received instruction in class on the mysteries of sexual interaction from none other than Ocky, the geography master, muscular Christian and amateur naturist.

Many years later it might be said that the dog-eared "French postcards", probably had a mildly traumatic effect on a few boys. Perhaps they could also be credited with causing others, as grown men, to behave with a degree of gentility. Most of my school-friends would surely have removed their hats and striped socks before indulging in adult boudoir-sports.

In those days, social mixing amongst adolescents was allowed, and even actively encouraged to some degree. Nevertheless, the old custom of chaperoning the young was still very much in force. In the opinion of some contemporaries, the rather sedate dances held in the school hall now and then were ruined by the close supervision of proceedings by teachers and parents. One or two schoolmistresses, generally slightly hirsute of upper lip and robust of physique, patrolled the gardens immediately adjacent to the hall, torches in hand, throughout the evening.

Surprisingly perhaps, given the revelations of misbehaviour by scoutmasters, sports coaches and, in particular, religious Brothers, Priests and Imans in many countries, no accusations of either physical or sexual abuse within the school in Cape Town ever saw the light of day in my time. Perhaps this was because there was a stern, rather Calvinistic, regime in place or simply that no one was inclined to complain. The productive industries of victimhood and the fruitful compensation culture were yet to come.

It was so, however, that boys attending the annual inter-schools cadet training camps were advised not to visit the tent of one of the officers directing the project. Captain J.J. Lamprechts taught at a high-school in a poorer part of the city and always attended these junior military camps. The Captain was a one-eyed, theatrically effeminate man, generally referred to with the derogatory adjective "Moffie" preceding his surname. This word actually describes fingerless gloves or a poorly bred sheep in Afrikaans. When used as in "Moffie Lamprechts", however, it means a rather effete or "camp" individual with a total lack of interest in ravishing members of the opposite sex. Of course this is a way of life no longer remarkable in the modern day world.

According to legend, Lamprecht's opening gambit when gaining the confidence of a young cadet would be to remove his glass eye, place it on his knee and discuss its provenance. Presumably he had an imaginative and carefully crafted story to tell at such exciting times. Whether he had in fact lost an eye in an unfortunate accident or on the front lines at Tobruk or Alamein, we never heard. The poor fellow passed into history uncelebrated but also without doing any real harm, possibly very much to his own regret.

These days, exactly how the young cope with the demanding appetites of puberty are probably still not a general topic of conversation in polite circles. On the other hand, at school, the ingenuity of a few miscreants in this area was the source of unbridled ribaldry and amusement to callow youngsters and, naturally enough, one of despair to those Calvinistic evangelists on the teaching staff who evidently believed that sex, rather than the love of money or of power, was the root of all evil.

One of the most peculiar boys circulating in those days was an overweight, fussy, and blatantly camp fellow whose parents ran a successful watermelon farm. "Rumble" Resnikow was so named because of the loud and unmusical sounds that emanated from the direction of his abdomen after any of his frequent visits to the school tuckshop. The flood of testosterone that was released into his body at the age of 14 or 15 did not result in any impressive muscular development or in a desire to indulge in violent sports such as rugby football. Instead, rather like his elder brother Selwyn, he remained flabby and sedentary but developed a quite bizarre interest in the over-ripe melons to be found in the more isolated corners of the paternal farmland. Not as a supplement to his diet, it must be explained. Embracing a watermelon is not subject to prosecution, at least not in any country of which I am aware. Furthermore, consent on the part of the fruit is not required, though a Melon Defence League might yet spring up somewhere, led perhaps by a new minority-group of misfits who identify as melons.

On the same theme, it is just possible that the two Resnikows were born well before their time, given present-day woke approaches to gender. Watermelons as surrogate lovers are, after all, non-binary and can legitimately be referred to as "they", if not one at a time then certainly in general. How dull of us not to recognise at the time that, far from being harmless perverts, Rumble and his brother were harbingers of a bright new democratic and diverse world to come!

When last heard of, Rumble was working in what is now rather grandly called "the hospitality industry". In other words he and a very close, slightly older, male friend of sensitive nature were running a bijou bed and breakfast establishment in a famous Western Cape tourist resort. The signs were that he had moved on from his unusual interest in slightly over-ripe watermelons. Brother Selwyn disappeared into the obscure ranks of the respectable and inoffensive folk that once worked on the front desks of post offices or banks, unsuspected of any deviant pass-times.

During the 1950s, the lives of children aged between 12 and 18 or 19 were organised almost entirely by adults. A fairly strict routine of lessons and sports was followed throughout the year, at least on weekdays. In the suburbs there were other organisations, unconnected to schools, providing after-hours activities designed (by well-meaning but perhaps humourless individuals) to keep youngsters out of trouble. *Inter alia* a touching belief seemed to exist that teenage boys and girls were less inclined to follow certain unseemly instincts prematurely if they could be kept chronically exhausted by vigorous physical activity. Of course, regular exercise and the fitness it produced merely increased the already flaming libidos of them all.

As part of this innocent approach to the prevention of moral decay, an earnest evangelical preacher, the Reverend Augustus Gainsborough, known as Gussy behind his back, founded a badminton club in our suburb, a few hundred yards from my home. During a period of slightly more than a year, about a dozen boys and girls in their mid-teens gathered there regularly on Tuesday and Thursday evenings. Four could be on the court at a time and the rest would be left to chat and amuse each other until their turn came to play. Everyone was dressed in white; tennis shorts and shirts in the case of the boys whilst the girls wore shorts or skirts that ended well above their knees. This was as it should be in the eyes of the innocent and pure; neat tidy and proper. The hall was opened and closed by any one of several adult volunteers, generally devout and kindly members of Mr Gainsborough's church, who were also charged with supervising the youngsters. The venture prospered at first but failed in the long term.

Once the evenings closed in and night fell at an earlier hour it became difficult for the adult in charge of activities to keep track of those club members not actually on the court. Even in winter, it was usually dry and warm; now and then a few of this group of healthy teenagers would wander outside.

The club was shut by Gussy after one of the young girls, a close friend of her mixed-doubles partner, began to put on weight at an alarming rate and, after a few months, left the youth club for a mothers-and-babies home run by a Catholic Sisterhood in another town. So, sadly, the Reverend Augustus Gainsborough's sortie into badminton as a form of family planning was not entirely successful. Nevertheless, he meant well and deservedly ended his career as a much respected elder of his church. There was never any word on what became of the badminton baby.

Much has changed in South Africa since those days and by no means all for the better. That is another story for a serious historian to tell.

UNIVERSITY

The school in Cape Town was modeled upon late 19th century ideas of how education in Britain and her colonies should be delivered. The manners amongst pupils of the school were generally so uniform that even slightly non-conformist behaviour by the likes of Louis the Russian, his brother Gabe, Joey the Ginger or the occasional farmer's son was disapproved of. The virtues and vices commonly found in young boys were well represented, however. Certain Americans would have described the school, like many others in the Cape and Natal provinces of South Africa, as offering a typical WASP (White Anglo-Saxon Protestant) education. Such is an excellent tradition in my view and one that largely remains in place now that the school is multiracial.

The university, situated inland in Johannesburg, was quite different in that, even in 1956, students came from a wide variety of backgrounds. Meeting and working with the children and grandchildren of Jews who had escaped the Nazi holocaust or the Eastern European pogroms was a new and enlightening experience, as was attending the same lectures as the limited number of Africans, Asians and "Coloureds" who were permitted by the government to study at a "white university". Friendships did develop across ethnic lines but, understandably, students tended to mix with others of their own, or similar, cultures. Most of my friends were middle-class, English-speaking, boys who were also studying medicine or who were members of the university athletic club.

In the late 1950s at least half, if not more, of the students came from families with no past history of any university education. Their fathers were working men, such as mechanics, traders, farmers or clerks, married to women who would have described themselves as housewives. Both parents would have experienced the Great Depression and the trials of World War ll, when men from all levels of South African society enlisted to fight for the British Empire and its allies. Their views were conservative as a rule and believed that colonialism was beneficial to the peoples of Africa.

As is still the case today, many students considered themselves to have insights that were lacking amongst the older generation and to be far more open to liberal values than their parents. The vehemence of their naive views then, as now, was inversely proportional to the seriousness of their studies if not also to their intellect and mental stability. Certainly a significant number of students in all faculties felt very uncomfortable with the manifest unfairness of the apartheid system. Even so, in 1956, not even those studying for powder-puff degrees in the liberal arts would have had any interest in burning down libraries and would have regarded the ideas of the woke brigade today as absurd. Professional courses, such as medicine, dentistry and engineering were far too demanding to allow time off for immature attempts at changing the world. There was certainly some virtue-signaling emanating from those most involved in organizing street demonstrations against the government of the day but the now familiar claims of victimhood by dysfunctional members of one fringe group or another were few and far between. No one had anything at all to say about dyslexia, attention deficit syndrome or gender dysphoria. Wild, unkempt, hair and a generally dishevelled appearance were likely to be seen as evidence of some personality disorder or early schizophrenia and were not associated with any particular world view.

There were some amongst the male students whose interests lay beyond the lecture theatres, sports fields or the protest movement. Those with knowledge of classical mythology might identify them as *satyrs*, given the vigorous and single-minded interest they showed in the opposite sex. These fellows made a big impression upon the more inhibited majority who were less mature in their choice of diversions but, nevertheless, much entertained, for better or worse, by stories of sexual conquests and chivalrous failures.

My best friend Bernard was a hard-working student but also a spare-time *satyr* who operated wherever the young and pretty were at hand. A handsome, well-made, fellow he had a strange obsession with long-haired girls. When introduced to a young woman with the right credentials he would initiate a conversation which, though simple-minded in both form and content frequently bore fruit, to the astonishment and envy of his friends. Somehow he needed to indulge in very little grooming (a term not yet in use) and his unsophisticated approach yielded a satisfactory harvest.

Bernard drove about in a tiny foreign car, a Fiat Cub to be exact, that could just accommodate two average-sized adults sitting bolt upright, with room behind the seats for not much more than a slab of Cadbury's Milk Chocolate (available at any Greek-Cypriot corner shop, 11 pence). It did, however, have a roof carrier. On some clear, warm, evenings Bernard would fix an old-fashioned, large, flat, surfboard to the roof of the vehicle. At first, this seemed very strange behaviour, given that the city was perhaps 500 miles from the nearest beach. It proved, however, to be, if not a work of genius, a very useful practical solution to the problems presented by wet grass and a very small car.

After attending an open-air "drive-in" cinema or perhaps sharing a meal at some greasy-spoon café, he would drive his quarry to a suitably quiet spot nearby, perhaps a park. Once there he would take the surfboard off the car roof and lean it at a comfortable angle against the rear of the vehicle, providing a far more appealing surface for mutual heavy breathing than might the damp grass. This was impressive lateral thinking but perhaps he might just as well have simply kept a warm tartan rug tucked behind the seats to be placed on the ground when the need or what-have-you arose.

Since the university was situated in the approximate geographical centre of the country, hundreds of miles from the ocean, holidays on the Cape and Natal coasts were sought after by both families and individuals. No students had much money to spare. It was the norm, and perfectly safe at that time, for the young to travel to the seaside sharing the costs of transport with their friends or hitch-hiking and sleeping near the roadside.

Bernard was given his small second-hand car by his parents after a motorbike accident during our 4th year at university. We would make our way to the coast in it quite comfortably. However, before that day came, we would simply pack our fathers' old army knapsacks and arrange to be dropped at a spot four or five miles out of town to start the hitch-hike southwards. The distance to Cape Town by the shortest route was around 900 miles and this, with good fortune and the help of generous motorists, could be covered in about 3 days. Generally there would be a reasonable flow of traffic on the road until the border of a semi-desert in the Cape, known as the Great Karoo. Here, the flow petered out and cars were few and far between. The little rural villages were often more than 50 miles apart and the lands beside the road were mostly occupied by vast sheep farms. On several occasions we sat for hours in the sparse shade of thorn-trees on empty Karoo roads, kitbags beside us, watching the insects and lizards in the dust and hoping some kind farmer would soon pass by, stop and take us further towards our destination.

At night we would usually sleep in the open, 20 or 30 yards from the roadside, rising early next morning in the hope of being spotted by some sympathetic driver with room for two slightly disheveled and, probably, less than fragrant youngsters. To signify our respectability, Bernard would wear his brightly-coloured university blazer on these expeditions.

Twice on our travels we slept indoors and so were spared both the dew that generally soaked our sleeping-bags of a morning and the attentions of any nocturnal insects or more dangerous creatures bent upon sharing our warm sleeping-bags in the veld outside. On the first occasion we were dropped off near a small Karroo railway station by a well-meaning but slightly rough-hewn Afrikaner travelling salesman named Frikkie Pelser. Someone that kindly people might describe as "salt of the earth", He drove us perhaps 100 miles in his rather dilapidated car, talking throughout the journey whilst fortifying himself at regular 3 or 4-minute intervals from a large bottle containing a liquid of uncertain provenance.

Mr. Pelser informed us that this was a special mixture invented by his great-uncle Barnabus. He identified it, in Afrikaans, as "'n lekker mengsel brandewyn en coke, boetie", which is to say "a tasty mix of brandy and Coca Cola, little brother". This potion, he explained, helped him to concentrate on the lonely road, though we detected no signs that it improved his driving skills at all. It was probably fortunate that there was almost no traffic abroad that evening.

The station was in darkness, quiet and deserted, when we reached it. There was to be no sign of life that night until very early the next morning when an express train went rattling by. The waiting room was open and we sat down to eat the stale ham and cheese sandwiches that we had bought at a roadside garage earlier in the day. We washed ourselves, without much enthusiasm or attention to detail, in the trickle of very cold brackish water that came from a tap in the lavatory before spending the night secure and dry, dozing very uncomfortably on hard, wooden, benches. Gratitude for warm home comforts made a brief showing and we resolved to avoid ever becoming homeless and sleeping in the streets of some city one day.

Our second experience, which was of relative luxury by comparison with that nameless railway station, was also somewhere in the Great Karoo. We were given a lift by a tanned young farmer of about 35 summers, stylishly dressed in khaki shirt and shorts and veldskoen shoes without socks. We were passing the entrance to a small town late in the evening when he suggested we might seek shelter in the local police-station where one of his relatives was on night-duty.

Our benefactor drove us to the building and introduced us to the two officers as "twee oulike Rooinek seuns van die pad af". Roughly that could be translated as "Two nice English boys from the road". Neither of us considered ourselves English but such was the custom of the day; if you spoke English then English you were. The Afrikaner police were very friendly and probably quite pleased to be diverted from the business of trying to find anything of interest to write in their daily report book. It was a village that was probably never disturbed by anything or anyone other than the occasional disorderly drunk or a stranger looking for directions to an out-of-the-way farm.

Life was marginally more exciting for the rural constabulary just then, however. A general alert was in place because a young recidivist gangster by the name of Kosie Pretorius had escaped from custody and was thought to be on the run somewhere in the greater Cape area. When the conversation began to drag a little the attention of the two policemen was captured, by my cheeky suggestion that Bernard bore a strong resemblance to Kosie, the escaped convict.

It is probably foolish to risk joking with people of an entirely different background but luckily Karoo Afrikaners tend to be practical people, albeit with a rather deliberate sense of humour. The Sergeant produced a photograph of the fugitive and observed that there was probably nothing much in common between Kosie and Bernard, beyond a head of hair and an arse (as he suavely put it). He thought it might be of significance that the wanted man stood only 5 feet and 3½ inches in his OK Bazaars cotton socks whereas Bernard was at least seven inches taller. So the matter rested there.

Once we had passed whatever tests of character the police applied, we were shown to an unoccupied cell where we spent a very quiet and comfortable night. As far as can be recalled, the door was left open and we had free access to the lavatories.

We were woken next morning by the younger police officer, a well-built, smiling man of roughly our own age who brought us coffee and rusks on a small tin tray. A far cry from the usual depiction of white policemen as genocidal maniacs made popular in leftist circles after the admittedly unforgiveable shootings at Sharpeville just two or three years later.

There is no record of what finally befell the small, but perfectly formed, desperado, Kosie Pretorius.

MEDICAL SCHOOL

The medical school that I attended after leaving high-school was on a hill outside central Johannesburg and some miles from the main campus where other university faculties were housed. From time to time, parties of medical students would venture "down the hill" to participate in such activities as interested them. In general they were too busy working through the vast medical curriculum to bother with the issues that excited the relatively idle, neurotic, liberal arts students. The latter were free to express themselves and to debate the issues of the day without being silenced by one group or another of sensitive people who felt "threatened" by the opinions of others. This approach was far removed from the restrictive political correctness of the English-speaking world today. During serious debates or controversial lectures by visitors of one stripe or another, heckling and other relatively peaceful forms of dissent were certainly allowed but they were kept within civilized limits.

Medical school was close to different hospitals for whites and blacks and perhaps fifty paces, in different directions, from two popular venues; a home for student nurses and a "greasy-spoon café". The latter, known as "Werners", was run by a German family, said to be in recovery from the downfall of Third Reich. Nevertheless, there was no obvious ill-feeling between proprietor Hans Werner and the numerous Jewish students amongst his clientele. Not while there was a plentiful supply of cheese sandwiches anyway.

My best friends at the time, Bernard, Dogface Robertson and Neil Steele, were fellow Gentiles who attended the medical pre-clinical courses for two or three years before completing their studies at a dental hospital some miles away. We continued to mix socially and spend occasional holidays together during our days at the university and for many years thereafter.

It was barely a decade after the end of World War ll and in the years 1953 to 1955 the last few students who served in that war had graduated. Many of them had experienced the worst of the fighting in Italy and, in some cases, had witnessed and perhaps participated in appalling acts of inhumanity when they were no more than 18 or 19 years old. Returning to civilian life in their early twenties, they were obviously older than most of the other students who had come to university straight from their high-schools, full of self-importance but somewhat wet behind the ears. The veterans had little time for rules or etiquette and no respect for any professors or lecturers whom they considered diffident or effete. The university authorities tended to make allowances for these men, as indeed they should have.

The exploits of the old soldiers at the medical school became almost legendary though one suspects there was some degree of exaggeration at work. The professor of anatomy at the time, Raymond Dart, a tough Australian of formidable intellect, was particularly tolerant of their antics. He did intervene to stop unseemly activity on one famous occasion, however. Dart walked into the anatomy hall to find 4 of our heroes playing cricket between the dissection tables with a thigh bone and a testicle taken from one of the cadavers. After observing that the "ball" seemed to be showing signs of reverse-swing on a flat wicket, he suspended them for 5 days. For those who do not follow cricket, it should be explained that 5 days would be the normal duration of an international test match at Lords, Newlands or Sydney Cricket Ground.

Most of the war veterans went on to become first-rate doctors. A few abandoned their studies and all had left the medical school by the time I arrived there with my friends.

The teaching course at medical school was quite demanding and followed a strict agenda that seemed rational at the time and was, most likely, based on the traditions of the great Scottish medical schools, several of whose graduates taught in South Africa. Students had to memorise a vast number of facts to be regurgitated at examinations, whether they were of much practical importance or not. Later experience, at Oxford University, by way of contrast, was that teaching by rote was frowned upon and independent thinking and the challenging of current ideas were encouraged by mentors of both undergraduate and postgraduate students.

The first few years of study at medical school were devoted to anatomy and physiology, in other words learning something of the design and performance of the healthy human body. Supplementary practical lessons of a voluntary and consensual nature were provided by friendly students from the nearby nurses' home.

These basic subjects led, logically enough, to pathology and studies in the causes, progression and end results of many diseases. Some of this work involved the examination and understanding of a collection of prize pathology specimens kept in a museum and presented in glass jars and students were also taught to recognise some of the microscopic features of common diseases. Once or twice per week, every student was expected to attend routine post-mortem examinations carried out on the bodies of patients who had perished in the hospital during the preceding 24 or 36 hours. It would be no exaggeration to state that several of the pathologists and assistants, male and female, bore uncanny resemblances to the beings from the underworld depicted in classical paintings from the middle-ages. Most sane individuals found these necropsies distressing and a tendency to cope by means of gallows humour began to emerge amongst us. The least said of this, the better.

Soon enough, students who had survived the initial basic training moved on to the clinical years. Lectures still featured but much of the teaching was actually in a hospital ward or in a small side-room close by. Students were expected to learn by taking medical histories from cooperative patients and sometimes were allowed to examine them under the watchful eye of a consultant or less senior doctor. Highly motivated students tended to return to the hospital after the medical school had closed for the day and to spend time observing events in the casualty or outpatient departments.

Teachers at the medical schools of the day emphasised proper respect and consideration for all patients, whatever their background. Students were also told time and again that the priority of any treatment should always be "first, do no harm". They had to learn how to manage conditions that involved the most intimate parts of the human body and to find ways of approaching delicate matters in a manner that would minimise embarrassment to patients. There were differences of opinion on how best to deal with this.

Many medically qualified men and women simply accept the basic functions of the human body as perfectly natural and, in common with most other aspects of life, open to discussion and, at the right times, mockery and humorous comment. In their families, the questions of small children are usually answered truthfully, nudity is not treated as intrinsically sinful and there is no need for references to gooseberry bushes or storks. This general approach has been the source of a few comical moments in my own family.

On one occasion my elder daughter, then in her late teens or early twenties, emerged from a hotel in Ireland to be confronted by a rowdy group of schoolboys celebrating the finish of their final examinations. One, who was evidently tired and emotional (which is to say, drunk) staggered up to her, exposed himself and said "Wah-shatink o dat". Translated, he wished to know her reaction to the rather unimpressive sight of his manly tackle. Her immediate response was to say "Oh, my! That looks a lot like a penis, only MUCH smaller". Fortunately the doorman was nearby and was able to rescue and escort her away.

On another day, many years before the Irish incident, my 3-year-old was walking happily to the shops in Woodstock, near Oxford, with his mother when they happened upon an old lady coming in their direction. She was slightly stooped and making slow progress with the aid of a stick, stopping to rest for a few seconds every 20 or 30 paces. With rimless spectacles, cashmere scarf and an antique bespoke overcoat, there was a definite air of distinction and faded beauty about her. She was carrying a small grocery bag in her free hand.

Once they had reached her, the little fellow's mother asked if she needed any assistance. The stranger, who was very well-spoken, thanked her saying she could manage and was almost home by then anyway. At this point our 3 year-old hero, who had been studying the old dear closely, felt it was time to join the conversation. "My daddy has a penis", he volunteered as an opening gambit. She looked into the distance for a moment, as if considering the importance of this information or perhaps enjoying the briefest of trips down memory lane. No doubt, she would not have known much about the frank exchanges that are usual in many medical families.

Her response a few seconds later was too soft to be heard but might well have been something along the lines of "I expect he does, dear" or perhaps even "more is the pity". As it was, there did seem to be a slight spring to her step as she left them and resumed her walk home. As it turned out, she was the relict of a local baronet and lived alone in a house a few yards from our own front door. Though we hardly ever caught sight of her again during the next two years, she made a point of wishing us well when our stay in the village ended. Lady Barnard was a rather typical genteel and reserved English lady.

THE CASUALTY DEPARTMENT

Even as a very junior doctor, it was possible to supplement the family income by working, after office hours, in what was then called a Casualty Department in one of the three or four hospitals that were within easy reach of home. These institutions included a large city hospital reserved for "Europeans", meaning whites, and a smaller hospital that catered for the black population living in the segregated townships near to Johannesburg, of which Soweto was to become the most famous.

At the whites-only city hospital, the casualty centre was where ambulances brought emergency cases and patients who had not been referred to a specific outpatient clinic by their family doctor. It was served during the day by fulltime medical staff and directed by a gentle and softly-spoken chief, Mr. Wilkinson. A Fellow of the Royal College of Surgeons he had evidently been forced to retire from fulltime surgical practice by a physical disability, possibly a complication of poliomyelitis. He ran a most efficient service that would be the envy of many such centres in the modern hospitals of Britain and Ireland.

Until about five or six in the afternoon, all the facilities of the hospital were fully operational. Specialised medical and technical staff were available all day to support and, if need be, advise their less able colleagues working in what would now be called an Accident and Emergency (A and E) department. In addition to dealing with minor medical complaints or referring incoming patients to various specialised outpatient clinics, A and E was the main portal for acute admissions to the hospital wards.

After six in the afternoon, fulltime medical staff would go home and be replaced by part-time doctors who worked for between one and three shifts of about four hours until eight in the morning. A full complement of nurses would remain on duty throughout the night. Most of the night-shift doctors were young and employed elsewhere as locums or, as in my own case, postgraduate research. Some were studying at home for much of the week, hoping to pass various entry examinations that might ultimately lead to their formal training and registration as specialists, most commonly in surgery. Others were simply marking time, deciding what path to follow. All were thankful for the opportunity to earn an extra income under not particularly demanding circumstances. The part-timers and the patients that attended the city A and E department both played a significant part in my own informal, unstructured and perhaps uncalled-for, further education.

On most evenings, the medical staff on call could be found drinking tea and chatting in the doctors' sitting-room as they waited for patients to be interviewed by a clerk at the front door and brought into the body of the clinic itself. A triage nurse would assess the urgency of any new arrivals and interrupt tea if need be. Obvious emergencies would usually arrive by ambulance, siren at full volume, and be moved straight into the emergency room without interference by the clerical staff. Leaving anyone waiting in an ambulance for hours was unheard of and would not have been tolerated. Somewhat dissimilar to the situation in the failing British National Health Service with its hundreds of directionless, medically-unqualified, inept and largely witless managers.

I recall working with friendly, slightly older, doctors who were invariably kindly and tolerant of their naïve young colleague, if not always so forgiving of each other. Most were 5 or 6 years my senior and, though South African citizens, all were foreign. Their number included a man from Lebanon, two Cypriot Greeks, a Portuguese from Madeira and a fiery Jewish Communist of Lithuanian origin. The friendlier of the two Greeks, named Dennis, was a bald-headed blond fellow with a slightly dramatic air, a tendency to wear colourful silk cravats and a libido directed quite exclusively towards his own gender. A nice man, he was said to be a talented pianist and was distinguished from us, his coarser colleagues, by his horror of rugby football, South Africa's violent national sport. It seems likely that his dislike of the game had to do with its inherent nature rather than with any objection to its clean-limbed, male, practitioners. None of us ever heard him play the piano and I have no idea whether he lived to become a leading light in the LGBT alphabet-soup movement.

Chris, the Lebanese was his polar opposite. He was given to taking me aside to warn me to beware of Dennis, to express his slightly biased, if not altogether unreasonable, opinion of the Communist or to share news of his recent conquests. He was a swarthy, well-made, healthy, chap, popular and much in demand it seemed by at least some of the comely members of the gentler sex who provided the nursing and other supporting services at night. His favourite seemed to be one of the radiographers, a pretty and intelligent girl named Penelope. Perhaps they shared an interest in philately or even philosophy, rather than in philandery; I asked no indiscrete questions. On the other hand, since Chris was a Lebanese Catholic, he might not have shared the conviction of some of his fellow countrymen that intimacy with 70 or more virgins awaited him in Paradise. So he took his chances as they presented themselves in this life. Chris has long-since passed on, so we shall never know.

Doctors in the casualty ward were actively supported by colleagues on the full-time hospital staff, chiefly in the medical and surgical wards, who would be "on take" (open to admitting patients) on any particular week-night. When one of us believed that someone should be transferred to the wards, a registrar of the appropriate specialty would be summoned to examine the patient and, if he agreed with the casualty assessment, arrange immediate admission. The registrar would normally be someone with 3 or 4 years of clinical experience behind him and might also have passed the difficult college examinations required to become a specialist in surgery or internal medicine. Most treated the Casualty staff in a civil enough manner and were tolerant of any errors their less experienced colleagues made in diagnosis. A few tended to be irritable and patronising; these were usually unfinished would-be surgeons, who were inclined to imitate the grand and dismissive manners they learned from some consultants. Strangely, candidates for a career in surgery often came from amongst those who once, as boys, liked to put together model aircraft with glue or to skewer and frame collections of butterflies.

On most evenings at the whites-only hospital we dealt with minor injuries resulting from household accidents and with the occasional heart-attack or stroke. The injuries were stitched, bandaged or immobilised in plaster-of-Paris, as required, and the life-threatening cardiovascular events handed over to the care of hospital physicians.

Now and again the scene would be enlivened for a short period by the arrival of a patient who was mentally deranged. Such patients could be schizophrenic or manic individuals who had been discharged from an asylum prematurely or had failed to take their medicines for a while. Some were simply foolish youngsters who had thought it worthwhile to add to the gaiety of a night out by mixing cane spirit or brandy with marihuana. Nearly all these people responded well to large doses of a powerful tranquilliser, injected by syringe into the muscles of their behinds. By morning they would be calm and ready to go home or to be returned to their regular medical attendant's clinic for further care.

On one occasion those of us on duty came face-to-face with an unpleasant reminder that hedonism and the swinging society of the time were not all a matter of wine and roses.

A polite, bespectacled, Afrikaner Calvinist of about 65, worked in an open-plan office, just by the entrance to the casualty ward. His job was to interview new arrivals at A and E who were not obvious emergency cases and to enter their details on a card that they would then hand to the sister on duty. This would contain a few details such as name, age, gender, main complaint, income and, where relevant, fees to be paid. There was an income-linked, graded, system of charges in operation. On most evenings, Mr. van Jaarsveld's duties would be undemanding and he would spend most of his time drinking coffee, reading his copy of *Die Transvaaler*, an obedient Nationalist newspaper, or dozing and perhaps dreaming of becoming a well-paid government senator.

One evening, at about midnight, the casualty department was disrupted by an extraordinary spectacle. Mr. van Jaarsveld suddenly appeared, jinking and dodging between the benches in the central waiting area at an impressive speed and waving an admission card in one hand, shouting for help. He was being pursued by an extremely nimble, determined-looking, entirely naked, young woman. She seemed to be totally unconcerned about her nudity or surroundings and was evidently bent upon embracing the unwilling or perhaps terrified Mr. van Jaarsveld. Once the members of the astonished audience had recovered their equanimity to some extent, she was cornered and held still by two of the more athletic and robust nurses. Not particularly dismayed by being immobilised, she set about complaining at the top of her voice that nobody, including her main quarry, Mr. van Jaarsveld, seemed interested in taking advantage of her generous offer of immediate sexual gratification. Once she had been captured and subdued to a degree, a blanket was wrapped about her and she was sedated by injection of a suitably large dose of tranquilliser.

It would take a very po-faced or repressed individual not to see the humour in the situation. There was, however, a sad truth behind this display which we learnt in the next day or two.

At that time an interesting, if brazen, woman named Mrs. Phyllis Peake owned one or more seedy nightclubs in the city. To be brief, these acted as a front for prostitution. Men who visited the "clubs" could expect to be entertained by girls with whom they would first share drinks sold at highly-inflated prices. It was claimed by Mrs. Peake (as she was always referred to in the newspapers) that anything and everything else that might occur later was strictly between the "hostess" and the client. Pigs fly, of course. The girls received a very small basic wage and a percentage of the profits on alcohol bought by the men. Madam collected the lion's share of the money earned in any subsequent transactions between hostess and client; she managed her empire ruthlessly, robustly denying any wrongdoing when interviewed. Mrs. Peake also operated a sort of introduction agency, ostensibly for "lonely hearts", and later a visiting service for men in need of what was rather primly referred to as "relief".

Like the celebrated Cynthia Payne of London, her clients included judges, magistrates, priests, businessmen and, at least in Phyllis Peake's case, police chiefs. Not exactly a road less travelled.

Of course some worldly women were quite happy to become "hostesses" in this way but other, naïve, girls were sufficiently innocent to imagine that Mrs. Peake's businesses offered no more than a ready source of pocket money. Far from it. In any event, the Casualty patient was one of those who had once been an ingénue but had become sadly traumatised, confused and corrupted by the degenerate lifestyle in which she found herself. Alcohol, occasional drug-abuse, shame and rejection by her family had proven too much for her and the display in hospital that night was one of fairly classic mania. She was institutionalised and treated for her mental illness for some time. Her ultimate fate is unknown but the cause of her torment, Mrs. Peake, still prospered on the fringes of society some 30 years later. The oldest profession, of course, continues to flourish everywhere. A victimless crime or not even a crime, some insist but certainly an illustration of the commercial principle of supply and demand.

Work in the Accident and Emergency centres of black hospitals was quite another matter. These were indeed Casualty Wards and, at times, front-line surgeons from the World Wars might well have found themselves at home there. The essential facilities and the expertise of the doctors on call were about the same as those that existed in the whites-only hospitals. It was the number of patients being attended to at any one time and the range of their ailments that differed. This was naturally much to the disadvantage of the patients.

On an average evening in the so-called "European" hospital most admissions would be for diseases of affluence and excess connected with alcohol and tobacco together with the occasional aftermaths of motor accidents, suicide attempts and the inevitable strokes and organ failures associated with old age. All the doctors became expert at gastric lavage, the messy procedure of washing overdoses from the stomachs of depressed would-be suicides and drunken men and women. Nevertheless, there was generally a fairly relaxed atmosphere with plenty of time for a cup of tea between patients.

Attending to black patients whilst on accident and emergency duty, at least in those hospitals catering largely for Zulus, was a quite different experience. There would be an almost continuous stream of bloodied men, and more rarely women, admitted to the unit. The commonest injuries were scalp lacerations inflicted by blunt instruments such as sticks, the occasional half-brick or perhaps a glass bottle filled with water. These wounds almost invariably required cleaning, stitching and dressing as well as a routine anti-tetanus injection. All of which procedures were time consuming and meant there was nearly always a backlog of patients waiting on benches to be patched up. There would also be life-threatening injuries such as dangerous penetrating stab wounds, depressed fractures of the skull delivered by traditional, hard-wood knobkerries and now and again the odd bullet wound. All of the patients with serious injuries would be resuscitated where necessary and referred for emergency surgical care.

When questioned, most of the black patients seemed to know their assailants surprisingly well and were as phlegmatic about their injuries as a modern professional rugby player might be about his. There was no referee in evidence to hold up red cards for foul play however. The stock reply when a man was asked why "my friend" or "my brother" had assaulted him was "he did it for his pleasure". This was a euphemism for "just because he felt like it". In general, these patients were grateful and respectful though there were exceptions when devilish alcoholic brews had been taken. These casualty wards were decidedly not an ideal environment for the sensitive, the poetic or the ultra-liberal theorist.

Of course much has surely changed over the last five decades and probably the characteristics of patients and the manners of those caring for them have been affected by many influences. The least attractive of these has surely been a huge growth in feelings of entitlement amongst certain members of the public. This has led, in Britain and Ireland at least, to patients with minor complaints (that could easily be self-medicated with over-the-counter remedies) continually bothering general practitioners and choking casualty departments to the detriment of everyone else. Interesting that the stock response by politicians to the situation in both Africa and Europe has tended to be that there is no shortage of doctors and nurses, simply an unreasonable increase in the demand for services.

All things considered, one must assume that many, if not all, the main actors at the accident and emergency departments of my time are long gone. I hope some of them, if not all, had happy and fortunate lives in the end. Certainly, where the medical staff was concerned and as the wretched British politicians and their media spokesmen love to say, when they wish to avoid taking responsibility for past actions, *lessons were learned.*

Unfortunately, we are seldom told exactly by whom these lessons have been learned. Certainly not by the army of talentless bureaucrats that western society has spawned; the problem lies in far too much "management" and not enough "boots on the ground". We need more doctors and nurses and to allow them to captain their own ship.

CONSULTANTS

These days, doctors working in the British National Health Service include a number of vocal activists who seem to regard their duties as similar to those of train drivers, miners or postmen. When looking for salary increases they are prepared to go on strike and the hell with who bears the consequences. A generation ago, such was not the case, at least not to the same extent. The medical profession was home to many practitioners with a compassionate and altruistic approach who put their patients' welfare first, sometimes at the expense of their own families. Certainly, both before and after qualification as a doctor, I met many such dedicated individuals.

People with an inside knowledge of medical practice can confirm that the range of neuroses, personality defects and even psychoses within the profession is quite similar to that found amongst the population at large. Doctors are mostly decent people but their numbers probably include just as many vain, incompetent, mercenary, deluded, careless and criminally inclined individuals as any other group of professionals. Of course that excludes journalists and politicians amongst whom some or most of these characteristics are common enough if not a basic requirement.

At medical schools in South Africa and Britain during the late 1950s there was a very clear distinction made between students and teachers; the respect, and indeed deference, with which the consultants expected to be treated definitely bordered on the comical. This was absurd, given that all of them were simply men, and sometimes women, who had been gifted with reasonable intelligence and the ability to discipline themselves during their years of training. Whatever the customs of the day, students and junior doctors would always address senior staff either as "Sir" or "Professor" as was deemed appropriate. Nursing staff were expected to do the same, at least in public, and, within the teaching hospitals, matrons and ward sisters ranked well above students and interns in the hospital pecking-order.

One consultant amongst our teachers believed in an absolutely poker-faced approach to his work with patients. He would not tolerate laughter in his clinics and rebuked nurses who smiled by saying "decorum, sister please, decorum". Zero tolerance. On one occasion he led a group of trainees, gathered around the bed of a surgical patient who had entertained himself a day or two earlier by inserting a matchstick into his urethra. Whatever his motivation, the item became impacted and had to be removed by a urologist. The history of this slightly absurd event was provided respectfully by one of the junior doctors at the bedside. When a straight-faced wit in the back of the group asked whether, after inserting the match, the patient had experienced the stock symptom of "burning on micturition" two students laughed. Both were immediately expelled from the ward by the self-important consultant. Far better, surely, to have been less prim, smiled a little frostily and explained the joke to the patient.

Several times each year, at medical school, there would be a slight relaxation of protocol. During their training, students were divided into groups of about a dozen, called "firms", and were allocated by rotation to particular hospital wards for several weeks at a time. There they might be expected to perform menial tasks allocated by the ward sister, attend teaching sessions conducted by the consultants and also to interview and examine patients whilst under the supervision of the junior doctors.

When the time came for a student firm to move on to another section of the hospital, say from a medical to a surgical ward, a small celebration would take place to mark the end of a particular teaching period. This would nearly always be in the form of a dinner-party held in the home of one of the wealthier students and would be attended by nursing and medical staff, often including the main consultant or "Chief", as he was known. Some of these firm parties were quiet, civilized, and unremarkable but, more often than not, heroic quantities of alcohol would be consumed by all and an unusual bonhomie and familiarity developed between guests of different status as the evening moved on.

One of the harshest consultants, a surgeon with a reputation for throwing instruments in theatre and reducing nurses, if not students, to a state near to nervous collapse was a man in late middle-age named Eliot Huggett. A ginger-haired, freckled, slightly overweight, man of average height and with a loud, unpleasant voice and jarring accent, he was from Sydney, Australia, and had moved to South Africa after being divorced by his second wife. It would not be unkind to describe him as someone who was feared rather than respected. Certainly he was unloved and students avoided him whenever possible. The only person who seemed to be a match for him was his ward-sister, Marcia Black, a woman of impressive physical proportions. She was what used to be referred to by an older generation as "a goddess". What the celebrated late British comedian, Benny Hill, would be inclined to describe, with mock relish, as "a BIG woman".

Like all mankind, Eliot the surgeon had his Achilles heel. In his case it was that certain beverages, of which he was quite fond, tended to interact with his unusually high circulating levels of testosterone and, reducing his self-control, lead him into situations that he might have cause to regret later.

On one occasion, several of my student friends and I attended a firm party held to mark the end of our spell on this man's ward. The beautiful home in which the party was held had spacious, well-furnished reception rooms and offered a large table, laden with both food and strong drink. French windows opened to lawns and a rose-garden, enclosed by a stone wall, the whole discreetly floodlit after dark. Jackets were discarded as the evening passed by and the bold Huggett becoming visibly more relaxed with each drink, could be seen engaged in smiling, animated conversation with some of the nursing staff. It might be stretching a point too far to suggest that he was becoming ebullient but he was also seen to speak to one or two of the students, something which was well beyond his normal social repertoire.

After a few hours, and when everyone had apparently had their fill of food and drink, the hosts brought in trays of coffee to be imbibed before anyone retreated to their cars. There was no sign of Eliot Huggett. That is, there was none until one of the students, looking through the open French window, spotted movement beyond in the rose-garden. An audience quickly, if unsteadily, gathered at the window to witness a disagreeable, if somewhat amusing, spectacle.

In amongst the rose-bushes, close to the stone wall, stood or, to be more accurate, moved an ill-matched couple. The esteemed Mr Huggett was in his expensive shirt-tails, trousers about his ankles, Y-fronts just below his knees and his anatomy exposed in far too much detail for any polite description. The state of Sister Black's clothing could not be clearly seen as she was partly obscured by the surgeon, his back being towards us. She was, it seemed, bracing herself against the wall and towered above him in the shadows as he worked away industriously at a lower level.

There was a brief outbreak of muted applause from the spectators but then the junior doctors present, fearful of future retribution perhaps, ordered everyone to remain quiet and detached, paying no attention to the couple if and when they returned from the garden.

Not a word was said when surgeon and ward sister reappeared at the coffee-jug. Both were flushed and somewhat rumpled; a high heel on one of Sister Black's fine shoes (Garlick's January sale, £8) was fractured and she limped slightly. This story was told repeatedly in the medical school over the next five years, often suitably embellished and always to the great amusement of the clinical students. Mr Huggett was treated with the same reserve and caution as before but his juniors never felt quite as cowed or disadvantaged from that time on.

Imaginative television series about hospitals seldom depict doctors and nurses as they really are. Breathless radio and television interviews involving medical academics, often present them as infallible experts in the very aspects of medicine they know least about, and reinforce the absurd idea that these men and women differ in some profound way from the general run of civilised humanity. It would be astonishing if more intelligent members of the public did not feel alienated by some of the medical men who advised governments on every aspect of the Covid-19 pandemic. Some of these off-key "experts" presented forecasts based on false extrapolations of non-existent data and advocated harmful lockdowns that had catastrophic effects and saved few, if any, lives. These "experts" proved that any differences that might exist between doctors and other professionals in self-awareness, hubris, narcissism and other neuroses are small and unimportant. Some, in Britain, were rewarded for their services with knighthoods, a form of recognition best avoided by anyone wishing to avoid being mocked or mistaken for a gender-neutral pop-star or retired sportsman of some kind.

THE GARDEN OF EDEN

During the years from 1971 to 1991 I lived with my wife and young family in what was then the province of Natal, South Africa. The country was governed by stern Afrikaner Calvinists in what they saw, primarily, as their own best interests and, secondly, that of all the country's different peoples. Perhaps the Nationalists were not entirely without their redeeming virtues, if changes in that land since the year 2000 are taken into account. Back in the "bad old days" South Africa was amongst the top dozen or so trading nations and had an excellent infrastructure that supported policing, adequate hospital services, a reliable electricity supply and food production (both with a surplus for exports abroad), schools, roads, postal services, railways and airports. Unfortunately, although there was a beneficial "trickle-down" effect, these services were provided unevenly (though just about adequately) to rich and poor, black and white. There was also religious tolerance; a vanishing commodity in the brave new world, led as it seems to be by backward immigrants and European or American individuals belonging to the largely certifiable liberal left.

Sadly, governance was accompanied by mean-spirited, unyielding segregation and a lamentable failure by some whites to recognise the dignity and valid ambitions of ethnic groups other than their own. This attitude, it should be said, originated in an understandable desire on the part of most Afrikaners to protect their own culture and people, many of whom had lost almost everything in consequence of the Anglo-Boer War. To an extent, for historical reasons, both blacks and "the English" were still regarded as "enemies of the blood" in the late 20th century though any violent clashes with the latter had been largely confined to the rugby fields once the South African war ended around 1902.

Many white families lived in fine style during the 1970s and 80s. Some still do, behind their security fences and closed-circuit television cameras. Most homes in the suburban villages were set in at least an acre of land, well back from the street and shielded from noise and the summer sunshine by trees and hedges or walls. Being in the southern hemisphere, the main aspect of houses tended to be north-facing. Most middle-class homes would boast carefully tended lawns, a few trees and shrubs, perhaps a flower-garden and, ideally, in view of the humid summers and all-year sunshine, a swimming-pool. There would be space nearby for comfortable chairs to accommodate family and friends enjoying ice-cold lagers and steaks from the built-in barbecue. The main house would often be air-conditioned but, at that time, security-systems were still in their infancy. Decorative bars on downstairs windows sufficed to keep out burglars other than the occasional impudent little grey monkey looking for fruit.

Our home was perhaps 20 miles from the coast, about 700 feet above sea-level in a quiet, wooded area. Beside the house there was a small copse, made up of perhaps 100 tall indigenous trees. Tree ferns thrived in the shade and there was a small perennial stream running through the wood to eventually drain into the great natural gorge that lay some two or three miles to the east. A variety of beautiful creatures were native to the area and could be seen in the woodland, regularly if they had made their home within it, less commonly if they just visited in search of food.

Over the years, incredibly, more than 100 species of birds were identified in the Meadow Lane garden, including the exotically named Paradise Flycatchers and Narina Trogons, four distinct types of Robins, four varieties of Cuckoo, two each of woodpeckers and owls and also the rare and mysterious Buff-spotted Flufftail. Something of a ventriloquist, the reclusive Flufftail had a mournful, ghostly call that seemed to come from somewhere below the earth. The Zulu tradition had it that the cry was not that of a bird at all but of an invisible, poisonous frog whose bite would fell an ox. Another song heard from the woods, generally after sunset, was that of the Wood Owls, calling in duet. A female would utter a short string of hollow-sounding, contralto, notes that were answered immediately by a single hoot from the male. According to Zulu informants, the female was offering herself at a price. This was "a-pound, a-pound-and-a-shilling", to which her would-be lover could only answer "wow!" These were strangely comfortable sounds in the evening gloom; the night music of a vanished paradise.

Any number of aloes and other flowering African plants grew near the house. These attracted three or four types of little sunbirds that fed on their nectar and two different forms of brilliantly coloured Halcyon Kingfishers that came to chase the insects disturbed by the sunbirds.

Vervet monkeys would regularly visit the trees in noisy troops of perhaps a dozen, raiding birds' nests and throwing half-eaten figs that the fruit-bats had ignored the previous night onto the ground. They were unimpressed by humans, whom they tended to ignore, but would lope noisily away if startled by a sudden loud noise or if they spotted a tree-snake in their vicinity. Now and then a huge Crowned Eagle from the rocky cliffs of the deep gorge a mile away would circle overhead and monkeys, the eagle's favourite lunch, would scatter at great speed, dropping from the trees to hide in the undergrowth.

The woods also sheltered other animals such as the charming native Genet, a handsome, little spotted wild-cat, the occasional small deer and various reptiles and amphibians. However, it was a creature from the original Garden of Eden and mentioned in Genesis 3 that caused most consternation during the 15 years we spent living in this mini-paradise.

On most days, after work at the medical school, down near the sea, I would return home and park my motor car, a rather nice German saloon, in a garage beside the house. This was separated from the indigenous woodland by no more than a rusting wire fence. Occasionally, due to idleness or the need to make an early start the next day, the locked car would stand outside until morning, close to the garage door.

One Monday at the end of summer, after leaving the car in this way, I drove to work as usual, and parked it in the hospital grounds, where it remained for much of the day. On my way home, at about 5.30 in the afternoon, I stopped for petrol at my usual filling-station near the university sports fields and was greeted by Robert Sindane, a fine Zulu pump-attendant whom I knew reasonably well. Sindane had seen perhaps 40 summers and was husband to several women and the father of many children. At heart he was definitely a Zulu of the old school. "How are you today, Professor", he said politely in his correct but heavily accented English. "Shall I check the water?" In the humid climate of Natal, cooling systems were constantly in need of appraisal so checking the radiator water-level was a standard procedure whenever a car was refuelled.

I released the catch securing the car's bonnet which Sindane then raised in order to make his inspection. He sprang back almost immediately and quickly returned to the car window, shaking slightly. "There's a big snake in there, sir!" he said.

I was unimpressed by this news, thinking that perhaps some harmless house snake had entered the car hunting for mice. There were also known Zulu superstitions concerning large snakes; some believed their organs had magical properties, yet others that some of these reptiles might harbour the spirits of long-dead relatives. Perhaps even one of a man's late 5 or 6 mothers-in-law! What could be more frightening? So I got out of the car and walked round to make my own inspection.

Curled at least twice around the cooling system of the car was an impressively large, disgruntled-looking, thoroughly unfriendly, black mamba. It is worth mentioning that these snakes, which are to be found in many parts of tropical and sub-tropical Africa, do not have a pleasant reputation at all. Black mambas are notably short-tempered and aggressive towards other creatures trespassing in their territory, particularly if the visitor happens to stray into the area seen to be an escape route by the snake. The bite of these reptiles, containing both nerve and heart poisons, will kill a grown man within a matter of a few hours unless the antidote is administered promptly.

It was whilst Robert Sindane and I were in earnest discussion about how best to dislodge the unwelcome stowaway that the first of two other players in the drama arrived at the petrol station. Wellington Ndhlovu was walking on his way to a bus stop nearby after completing his day's work at a small corner shop on the hill above us. A fine figure of Zulu manhood even at the age of about 70, he was immaculately dressed, in spite of the heat, in a three-piece dark-blue, pin-striped suit. He sported a black, battered, homburg hat and carried a tightly-rolled umbrella in one hand. This vision of sartorial elegance was slightly spoiled by the fact that he wore rather muddy, white tackies (as tennis-shoes were known in Natal) with threadbare laces. After politely greeting those present and enquiring after our general health, as is the Zulu custom, he surveyed the scene and suggested that the front of the car be raised with a jack and the snake sprayed with the contents of a portable fire-extinguisher, thus encouraging it to leave its roost.

This suggestion seemed reasonable at the time, given that neither of us had any practical knowledge of how to remove black mambas from German sedans and so followed the advice of our dignified new companion. The mamba reacted by baring its fangs and hissing at our nervous *ad hoc* trio, showing unambiguously that it was displeased. Aware that this particular snake was more dangerous in its own way than the serpent guarding the Tree of Knowledge and could well kill us, we retreated slightly to discuss whether there might be a viable Plan B.

At this stage, a new member of the supporting cast arrived, this time by car. Mr "Bakkies" van Tonder parked his Volkswagen next to one of the petrol pumps. Seeing the little group gathered around my car and being a small-time government bureaucrat, he decided to investigate and perhaps to advise us on anything at all. Mr van Tonder was a ruddy-faced, bulky individual of about 45, dressed in a safari-suit as many petty civil-servants did at that time. This consisted of matching pale-grey shorts, reaching to a hands-breadth above the knees, and a shirt with button-down pockets, worn over his belt. He also wore knee-length woollen stockings together with the rough-looking but comfortable shoes known in that part of the world as "veldskoene". It should also be explained that "Bakkies", derived from "baksteen" (meaning "brick" in Afrikaans), is a nickname given as a rule to hard-nosed rugby forwards or other individuals better known for their unyielding toughness than for their intelligence or sparkling wit. In the event, the new arrival was physically imposing and, having the familiar bearing of a petty official in government service, appeared worthy of his nickname. Perhaps he was actually someone with limited authority of the type referred to in England as "a jobsworth".

Bakkies addressed the three of us in Afrikaans with all the authority of a South African policeman or Dutch Reformed Church minister of those days. "What is going on here?" he said, in a tone he might use when discovering that someone had failed to complete some bureaucratic form correctly or was in a no-parking zone. The two black men looked uncomfortable and did not reply, recognising an approach commonly used by white officials when checking their identity documents or harassing black people in other ways. So I responded in his language and told him that there was a black mamba under the bonnet of my car. Understandably, perhaps, he received this news with disbelief, mambas not being known to make appearances at suburban filling-stations as a rule.

Just then the mamba, possibly tired of being discussed by the humans in no less than three languages, dropped to the ground and moved with great speed away from the garage forecourt and towards a refrigerated self-service machine for Pepsi-Cola and other refreshments that stood beside the garage building itself. Our newly self-appointed commanding-officer and leader, Baksteen van Tonder, observed this move and scornfully informed us that it was no mamba but "just a blameless mole snake, man". Nevertheless he stayed well out of its way. Of course it was certainly not a mole-snake and no black mamba was ever born that was either harmless or, for that matter, virtuous to the extent of being without blame. The body-language of the black men indicated that they were more uncomfortable in the presence of Mr van Tonder than in that of the mamba and that they were not impressed by his advice to ignore the snake. I resisted the temptation to inform him that I had studied reptiles at one stage and instead suggested, by way of compromise, that it might be best to leave the snake with the Pepsi-Cola tins in the machine. It would certainly leave the premises in its own good time during the night.

The two Zulu braves had far too much common sense to agree with either of their white advisers and, after a brief and animated discussion, decided that the mamba should be pulled by the tail from the machine, despatched with a blow to the head and sold to Elijah Msombalugu, the local Sangoma or witch-doctor. Msombalugu would, in turn, retrieve various magical parts from the dead mamba's body and market them at retail prices as cures for various ailments, ranging from urethritis to cancer or, at much higher prices, as a means to cast spells on potential lovers or enemies. Msombalugu would do this without bothering whether or not the snake had once harboured the spirit of someone's deceased mother-in-law. Cash turnover would take first priority. Such was indeed the mamba's ultimate fate but not until just before nightfall.

It was at about 6.15p.m., with the snake still coiled amongst the Pepsi-Cola cans, that Mr van Tonder remembered why he was at the filling-station in the first place.

Placing his horny hand heavily on Robert Sindane's shoulder and, speaking in English he said, "Listen boy, leave the snake now and just fill up my car wif petrol, hey." The response from Sindane was a classic and to the point: "Sorry sir, we close at six."

And there the story ends.

THE BOERS

There were a number of ethnic groupings in South Africa to which my family did not belong. The largest grouping of whites is still made up of Afrikaners, sometimes referred to as "The white tribe of Africa". These tough, durable people are mostly the descendants of Dutch, German and French settlers who came to the country in the seventeenth and eighteenth centuries. Some intermarriage with Britons and the regular, if occasional, donation of DNA by eastern Europeans and indigenous African and Indonesian races formed a distinct new nation with its own Germanic language and social customs.

A great deal that is less than complimentary has been written about these people, mainly by liberal leftists with their own agenda, petty jealousies and delusions. It goes without saying that few, if any, foreign critics of the Boers ever bothered to master their very expressive language or understand their cultural history and the direction in which it moved. That said, it is important to state that criticism of the apartheid regime imposed by Afrikaner politicians during the 20th century came from wider sources than just bearded academic theorists in sandals or from the unfortunate victims of the system. Much carefully considered and justifiable opposition to this evil policy came from righteous Afrikaners and from the South African press, which was free to a surprising degree. These critics were referred to as "verligtes", meaning *the enlightened ones*.

There is an alternative way in which to consider the sometimes self-destructive behaviour and nature of many 20th century Afrikaner patriots. A people with a strictly Calvinistic approach to life, they came to a largely empty sub-continent and suffered greatly in their efforts to tame the wilderness. They confronted and blunted armies of the mighty (and in many ways admirable) Zulu nation and did their utmost to frustrate the efforts of a number of greedy predators amongst the otherwise talented, latter-day, English settlers.

Around the 1830s the Boers, forefathers of the governing elite of the twentieth century, began moving north from the Cape of Good Hope to escape British influence and, in their quest for land, were soon involved in bloody fighting with various African tribes, notably the Zulus. Some of the black groups had established themselves in certain areas up to 500 years before this white migration, though others were still moving southwards into what became South Africa from further north.

Both Boers and blacks, it should be noted, were involved in the decimation, indeed genocide, of the true indigenous people of southern Africa, namely the Koi and San nations.

Newcomers from Britain settled in what would become outposts of their Empire at its peak. They occupied vast areas of undeveloped and largely empty land, initially farming and later building villages and towns and helping themselves to territories the Xhosa and Zulu considered to be their own. Roads, harbours, schools and hospitals were all constructed and the colonies along the coasts of the Cape and Natal were governed under the aegis of the Crown although not without significant bloodshed during the middle of the 19th century. The inland areas known as the Free State and Transvaal were governed by the Boers. Much later in the day, after rich sources of gold and diamonds had been discovered inland, British forces invaded the Boer Republics on the pretext of supporting the right to vote of a few hundred scruffy Englishmen living there. In fact, this was a sadly typical, hypocritical stroke, orchestrated by British metropolitan elites, motivated by greed and intent on taking control of the natural resources of Southern Africa. Prominent amongst these people was one Cecil John Rhodes. He was a man remembered, accurately enough, as a ruthless businessman and coloniser but who was also one of the first individuals to advocate enfranchising the Cape Colony population at large, irrespective of race or religion. He died young and so what he might have achieved living into late middle-age can only be speculated upon.

The Victorian Britons were truly admirable in many ways, most notably the wonderful feats of engineering they were responsible for in various countries. They also exported many of the gentler aspects of their culture to savage places. Unfortunately, too many influential individuals amongst them were arrogant, materialistic, hypocritical and unmerciful. So not much change over the centuries then!

As mentioned above, British forces invaded the Afrikaner republics, after making their mealy-mouthed statements about voting-rights for foreign adventurers. Of course those behind the argument were motivated by greed and envy, coveting land, gold and diamonds. Two Anglo-Boer wars resulted.

At first the invaders were a poor match for the Boers, who defended their homes with great courage and ingenuity. They knew the unforgiving terrain and were finer marksmen and better horsemen in the local conditions than any number of both the public schoolboys and enlisted men from poor backgrounds who made up the bulk of the invading forces. Eventually the kindly British generals, inspired by the adage *the end justifies the means* or perhaps *all is fair in love and war*, introduced disgraceful, amoral, tactics designed to destroy the source of supplies to the Boer irregulars. They burned down thousands of Boer farms and interned the occupants in concentration camps with disastrous results. Of an Afrikaner population numbering perhaps one quarter of a million souls, over 30 000 perished in the camps, almost all women and children. Most of them died of the infectious diseases that resulted from concentrating a largely rural population, with poor natural immunity, in relatively small spaces. The Boers were not amused by this interlude and an extreme Afrikaner nationalism was born. The British authorities and their supporters chose to "forget" their shocking behaviour and, in addition, invent scurrilous stories about the "uncivilized Boers" to justify the rape of their society. On the Boer side what we would now call "conspiracy theories", such as that the British had put finely ground glass in the camps sugar, flourished. Fortunately, in due course, the best of the ordinary people, Boer and Brit forged a noble peace and South Africa flourished.

It would be foolish to pretend that the Afrikaners were ever uniformly brave or noble though many of their leaders, particularly Smuts, Botha and de Wet most certainly were. Yet these farmers were made of steel and, once they had lost almost everything, made peace with their tormentors and ultimately worked with them and many of the native peoples to build a sophisticated western society. Even the great jingo, Winston Churchill, admired them and expressed the view that, at the time of the second Anglo-Boer War, the Afrikaners were, man-for-man, more than a match for the English. Echoes of his opinion can still be heard in rugby stadiums to this day, particularly when Scots, Irish, Welsh or South Africans settle old scores with England!

Sadly, after 1945, the desire to preserve their culture in the face of an ever-increasing black population gave rise to the segregationist policies of the Nationalist Government. Many ex-servicemen in Britain remained loyal to their old comrades and supported South Africa but this became progressively more difficult to sustain as former supporters of Nazi Germany, such as the odious J. B. Vorster and his friends, began to direct the country.

The younger generation in Britain's great cities knew little, (and knows even less now), of the heroic exploits of great, open-minded, Afrikaners such as General Dan Pienaar at Alamein or Group-Captain A. G. "Sailor" Malan during the Battle of Britain. Very few understood the underlying Boer fears of extinction which dated back to the English concentration camps of 1901-1902. The toothsome sandals and white socks brigade of liberal leftists and their media friends came into their own and the Boers were painted internationally as brutish and stupid, a stereotype previously reserved for the Irish and currently being applied to Israelis by the usual coalition of the malignant and the stupid. The same critics would be unaware that the words that follow were those of a white Afrikaner and undisputed war-hero, Sailor Malan DSO, DFC, when he co-founded the Torch Commando, in opposition to the mad apostles of apartheid:

We oppose the police state, abuse of state power, censorship, racism, the removal of the coloured vote and other oppressive manifestations of the creeping fascism of the National Party regime.

In response to criticism most white South Africans became defensive and, reasonably enough, compared their own country favourably with most African, Arab and East European nations. They dug their heels in and got on with the business of developing the infrastructure of the country to the benefit of much of the population. Whilst their efforts were successful in many ways, the policy was heartless in others and, at almost every level, failed to recognise and respect the dignity of individual people of colour, many of whom could have been assimilated into a single nation quite seamlessly.

Personally, I was privileged to make many friends amongst the Afrikaners although, as with every race, they are not and never have been a homogenous group of people. Some of that community would best be avoided. One needed a fluent understanding of the Afrikaans language to appreciate the robust, generally unfiltered, sense of humour of a people who were of the soil and were unafraid to be unmercifully direct in what they had to say. Deference to authority was in short supply and the teaching of that time was that a man bowed only before Almighty God. The varied nature of Afrikaner society in the 20th century might best be illustrated by comments relating to the most basic and the most elevated amongst them.

The tendency to avoid euphemism and petty politeness was, naturally enough, more marked in those members of the Afrikaner community who did not have the benefit of a rounded modern education. An example of their unpolished humour was provided by a close friend whose father was a senior member of a company that employed about 200 unskilled white individuals, packaging cigarettes. Each Christmas, the firm would entertain all its employees and their wives or partners to a candle-lit dinner held in a large space that had been specially cleared of all equipment for the occasion. The directors would stand at the door to greet each couple as they arrived, before handing them on to a steward of sorts who would direct them to their seats. A familiar enough situation perhaps, at least in some workplaces, with vaguely uncomfortable employees in their Sunday best, making efforts to appear relaxed and accustomed to what was set before them.

On one occasion, Voël van Jaarsveld, who worked at the factory, arrived for Christmas dinner together with two rather raffish-looking young women, one on each arm. Voël, which means "Bird" in polite Afrikaans but is otherwise a euphemism for a male organ that apparently is no longer gender-specific, was a renowned, if dim-witted and unsophisticated, ex-rugby player. His job was, at best, semi-skilled. The senior director recognised him and, meaning well but speaking to the girlfriends in a rather patronising manner, said:

"Wat het HY wat EK nie het nie?"

Translated from the Afrikaans, this means "What has HE got that I don't have".

One of the girls, neither of whom had attended a Swiss finishing school, responded immediately and possibly with a fair degree of accuracy:

"Hy het 'n groot, stywe, piel wat jy nie het nie!"

The exact meaning of her reply should best be left without going into too much detail given that, when directly translated, several of the choicer words amongst those she used were very crude synonyms for "enormous", "upstanding" and "dick". Put as smoothly as possible, her remark was in reference to the younger man's satisfactory sexual potency. This, based on her experience, would trump that of the chief executive who was, after all, at least 55 years old (and therefore terminally elderly to a 20-year-old ignoramus).

Lacking the self-importance that is so common amongst many little men in Europe, the director referred his slightly less than genteel guests to the steward with a broad smile and recounted the story with good humour for years afterwards. A joke that was probably far too unsubtle for most sophisticates raised outside the Teutonic countries where what passes for humour can be really quite regrettably crude.

On a couple of occasions one had the impression that at least some senior members of the Afrikaner establishment were less than convinced that the policies of their government were fair or fell within the broadest definitions of loving one's neighbour.

At one stage the teachers, nurses and doctors at the medical school and teaching hospital in Durban, Natal, were paid salaries that were determined by race. Thus, whites were paid more than Indians and so-called coloureds. Blacks were paid least of all. An outrage really, given that this was clearly disrespectful towards members of those races and a very deep insult to anyone amongst the "non-whites" who happened to be better qualified academically and more competent than some of their white colleagues. As a committee chairman of sorts at the time, I raised this matter with an amiable enough cabinet minister, who was visiting the province at the time. Dr Piet Koornhof was a charming Afrikaner, known by the English press as "Piet Promises" for reasons that can be easily guessed. At times he was depicted in satirical cartoons as Pinocchio, the Disney character whose nose kept growing each time he told a lie. In any event, Minister Koornhof, a man with a South African university degree in theology and an Oxford doctorate earned whilst a Rhodes' Scholar, listened to my arguments with great courtesy and apparent sympathy. In his youth, he had been a hard-line supporter of apartheid, but his attitude had softened and he promised to look into the matter, hinting that there would be trouble from his more doctrinaire colleagues. Nothing happened for a few years but, in due course, the policy was reversed.

Piet Koornhof must have been somewhat ambivalent about the racial policies of the government in which he served. He was eventually demoted for his dangerously humane views and ended his public life as Ambassador to the United States. At the age of 68, shortly after the release of Nelson Mandela, he left his wife for a younger woman of "mixed race", with whom he had several children. A few years earlier and the country's laws, set in place by his own political party, forbade inter-racial marriage and advocated imprisonment for "immorality" which was how sexual activity across the colour-bar was described. He spent his last years as an admirer of President Mandela and a member of the once respected African National Congress.

Minister Koornhof was by no means the only Nationalist grandee who had impeccable manners and a sympathetic ear. One needs to remember that governments make decisions in cabinet which means by achieving some sort of consensus amongst individuals who might differ in viewpoints, insight, compassion and common sense. Compromise of some sort is generally the outcome of committee meetings and compromise leaves almost as many casualties as open dispute; perhaps more evenly distributed.

On one occasion in the early 1970s I flew home from an international medical congress on the same aircraft as a middle-aged missionary of sorts, a Swiss woman of perhaps 60 summers. As far as I could determine, she was coming to work as a teacher, or possibly medical assistant, in a mission station out in the wilds of Zululand. When we disembarked in Durban there was considerable excitement. A large reception committee, made up of Zulu men, women and children, had travelled many miles by bus from the north of the province to greet her with their songs and bring her back to their place in the north. To my eyes it was a moving and beautiful welcome indeed.

This seemed to be an altogether delightful and happy scene, at least until one approached the crowd. There was an open area at the front of the airport terminal where whites could wait to meet their friends and families. The missionary's new congregation and friends were black and therefore segregated. All of them were kept together behind a tall diamond-mesh fence through which the smaller children thrust their hands, reaching out to her as she passed into the main building. It was a sight that filled me with shame and disgust; one that was certain to leave a deep and negative impression of South Africa on the mind of any interested and observant stranger.

The next day I wrote a letter to the Honourable Ben Schoeman MP, the Minister of Transport, recounting what had been witnessed and asking what rational reason there could possibly be for partitioning an airport arrivals area by race. It was pointed out to him that the English, for example, do not confine the Welsh or the French to specially reserved areas at airports and railway stations, even if they might secretly wish to do so. Furthermore, this stupid practice was further harming South Africa's already tarnished image. It was a very direct and angry letter.

After a day or two the images of joyful children and a benign perplexed Swiss missionary began to fade. To everyone's astonishment, the outcome of my impertinence was not a meeting with security police but an unexpected, conciliatory letter from Mr. Schoeman himself. As with Piet Promises, the Minister of Transport clearly would have preferred a kinder, more accommodating South Africa. The letter assured me that he saw the problem and would attend to it. He kept his word in so far as his colleagues allowed him to and ultimately the fence came down. Minister Ben Schoeman was a former railway-man from a humble background but he had a reputation for decency. He attempted on at least one occasion to bring about a softening of race laws and later on was defeated by extremist skulduggery in a party leadership election that resulted in the promotion of the lamentable and evil J. B. Vorster to the post of prime minister. A disaster for South African sport, *inter alia*.

Koornhof, Schoeman and others were thoroughly good men caught up in an impossible situation. There simply was no easy solution to the problems inherent in trying to reconcile the differences between vastly different racial groups. They did try. In my own experience, the Afrikaners were, and remain, a worthwhile, often lovable, people.

DURBAN MEDICAL SCHOOL. SPOOKS.

The medical college at which I taught for almost twenty years was founded by idealists and devoted to the training of candidates for the profession who, by virtue of their race, could not easily gain entrance to any of the country's so-called "white universities" each of which had a handful of black students. Accordingly, the student body in Durban consisted of Black Africans, together with the descendants of immigrants from the Indian sub-continent and a small number of people of mixed race. The teaching staff included doctors of all races, many of whom were opposed to both the system of apartheid and to the violence advocated by many adherents of the African National Congress. Sadly, but perhaps understandably, the school could be a tense place at times. Many of the students would have been unaware that we, when choosing to work amongst them, had all accepted salaries far below those available to us had we ignored their needs and taken posts elsewhere. Some, I believe, were simply suspicious of white people and took the view that teaching staff were part of a conspiracy against them that originated within the apartheid government. On the other hand, the security branch of the police force and their supporters appeared to believe that only a crypto-communist would want to be a party to educating blacks. It was a classic case of "damned if you do and damned if you don't".

Early in my medical career I had worked in places such as hospitals and goldmines that either served or exploited Black Africans but had little experience of or interest in politics. Interaction with intelligent members of races other than my own had been limited though I had been friendly with a fair number of Afrikaners, whose language I could speak, and with a handful of talented colleagues of different races to my own. So, when I began teaching at the medical school, I was mystified by the drama taking place behind the scenes.

One of my duties during the first year after my return to Africa from Oxford was to conduct oral examinations in pharmacology at the end of the third year of study. Most students needed to pass this rather intimidating test together with a written examination in order to be promoted to the fourth year. A minority performed so well, or so abysmally poorly, in the written paper that the oral became no more than a box-ticking exercise. I considered it cruel to prolong the agony of those who had no hope of passing and would generally just ask them some simple question such as "what do we use aspirin for" or "name two drugs used to treat tuberculosis". Such candidates were nearly always males. If my initial question was answered satisfactorily, we moved on to more difficult issues so that the candidate might be given a chance to redeem himself. Usually he could not.

During one of these orals, a student with a woeful academic record came for assessment. His name meant nothing to me and I began with the usual question, designed to let him down easily. To my astonishment and delight he answered this, and three or four progressively more difficult questions, perfectly. Here was an unusually able man, capable of solving problems by applying his limited factual knowledge logically. This was unexpected and a relatively uncommon gift amongst the students at large who had come from a background of learning by rote.

I awarded him a pass mark and made enquiries amongst my colleagues about him. When told that he was a political activist who spent most of his time attending meetings and agitating in public for an end to apartheid, I decided to have a word with him.

We had a brief discussion in my office during which I suggested that it might be wise for him to complete his medical studies before setting out on a serious political career. The title "Doctor" before his name would improve his bargaining power and gain respect for his views, however grudgingly, from the apartheid government. He was polite in his response although he did accuse me of being an unrealistic liberal, perhaps not realising that believing in fair play is common enough amongst conservative people. Of course he probably did not fully understand the rather ambivalent approach to South African society that many of us had. Basically this was to follow the directions of Jesus Christ (unknowingly in most cases) and "render unto Caesar" whilst doing what we could to help the socially disadvantaged in any way that we could within the constraints of an imperfect society. A comfortable and perhaps cowardly approach, I fear.

He left me promising that he would work harder but failed other key subjects and so was excluded from the medical school in accordance with the rules at the time. He went on to study law and became something of a thorn in the flesh of the apartheid government. He had brushes with the security police on several occasions before his final, fatal confrontation.

In my opinion, this young man could have lived to be a great asset to the country. As it was, Steve Biko died young. He was killed by the police whilst in their custody. Nothing much relating to his death was ever put before the South African courts, at least not in its immediate aftermath. In due course, certain aspects of his murder came before the national Medical Council.

The security police made their presence known at the medical school and evidently relied upon the information they obtained from various sources there. One such source was the janitor, a morbidly obese and unlovely man of limited education, who made it his business to wander about the school slyly studying the activities of staff members. His interest was especially awakened by any evidence of unseemly behaviour by anyone of fairly senior rank. Knowledge of over-zealous expressions of sexuality in someone's private office could be used to persuade the guilty parties to cooperate in spying on students or other staff members. What his success rate was like, I cannot say.

During the early years of the 1980s I was amongst a group of South African doctors allowed into the Soviet Union in order to attend, and contribute, to an international cardiac conference. This was an interesting experience and, after time in Moscow, Tashkent and

Samarkand, I was left singularly unimpressed by Russia and, in particular, communism. In fact the only highlight of my time there was a visit to the home of the great Christian writer Tolstoy. On my return home I found myself much in demand as a speaker at various lunchtime gatherings of businessmen, ex-servicemen and, on one occasion, politicians. The deliberately jovial way in which I slated and dismissed the miserable Soviet way of life was intended to be entertaining but was misinterpreted by some in my audiences who evidently thought my views indicated a pleasing degree of right-wing extremism. This interested both the security police and the country's most right-wing political party, the Conservatives.

After about my third such free-lunch, I was approached at the medical school, in confidence, by a fine-looking young Afrikaner whom I did not know. He turned out to be one of my very many fellow competitors in the annual 55 mile Comrades Marathon and also a Lieutenant in the so-called special branch of the police force.

Since I took no real interest in the political activities of students and certainly had no interest in spying on them, I don't think I was ever of any use to Deon. We did have pleasant enough discussions however and he supplied me now and then with publications by the African National Congress, most of which indicated that it would be a sad day for everyone in the country if they ever came to power. Even then, there was little, if any, evidence that they understood how to support and maintain the infrastructure of a modern state or that democracy and self-interested corruption might not be quite the same thing.

The way in which the authorities were prepared to act in those days was quite impressive and, indeed, frightening. An event at about that time helped motivate me to leave the country permanently. I had mentioned to my new friend the Lieutenant that I thought a certain colleague must be a double-agent working primarily for the government. I had reached this conclusion because the man in question had never been arrested or harassed by security forces and yet was quoted in the newspapers almost every week condemning the nationalist government and generally making inflammatory statements about apartheid. Deon fixed his pale-blue eyes on me and said "Oh! Do you think so?"

Two days later a bomb destroyed the entrance of the suspect's expensive house in a select suburb reserved for Indians. He and his family were very conveniently away for the day when this happened. No doubt this had the desired effect; the revolutionaries were impressed and if he was indeed a double-agent he continued to act as such until the system collapsed and he joined the African National Congress with much fanfare.

My views on Russia also brought a representative of the political extreme right to my door. The deputy leader of the Conservative party, a man named Clive Derby-Lewis, had heard of my ruminations on Communism and wrongly thought that I shared his view that the South African government was far too soft on racial-segregation and that a much stricter application of apartheid was called for. He was a very single-minded individual and believed that Communism, which was well represented amongst senior members of the African National Congress, was a vehicle of the Anti-Christ. He would not have known of the threats yet to be posed by political correctness, Islamic extremism and the liberal left.

Over a cup of tea, Derby-Lewis invited me to stand as a parliamentary candidate for the Conservative party. I thanked him for his invitation but said that, in certain respects, his party was far too left-wing for me. I did not believe in "one man, one vote" for any race or population group but that the right to vote should depend on certain strict criteria unrelated to sex or race. These qualifications would eliminate about forty-percent of whites then enfranchised, including some members of parliament, and give a voice to capable people of all races. A sort of non-racial elitism, I suppose. He left, confused.

I have no idea what befell Deon the Lieutenant, though he seemed to lose interest in me as a potential spy. Perhaps he heard that I gave extra tuition to a couple of students who had been detained without trial or charge and who had missed a full term of lectures whilst locked up.

Clive Derby-Lewis lost the run of himself and orchestrated the murder of the South African Communist Party leader, Chris Hani. His death sentence was commuted and he was paroled after serving 22 years in prison, dying of lung cancer shortly thereafter.

Archbishop Tutu's Truth and Reconciliation Committee pardoned many murderous acts committed during the apartheid era by wicked people that included terrorists and agents of the state. All were deemed to have acted with political motives, an approach allowing the end to justify the means. For some reason there was no absolution for Clive Derby-Lewis or his accomplice.

THE MEDICAL COUNCIL

It was whilst working as Professor of Clinical Pharmacology at the Durban medical school that I gained a broader perspective on the Afrikaner nationalist party. I met and dined with many of their establishment after becoming a nominated representative of my university on the South African Medical Council. Some of the members of this body, one that was supposedly the guardian of good and ethical practice by South African doctors, were elected by ballot of their colleagues. Others were directly appointed by the Minister of Health or nominated by bodies that were in sympathy with the policy of apartheid. Care was taken to ensure that a majority of members could be relied upon to support any measures the Minister of Health might put before the council. As with Russia today, a purely *faux* appearance of democracy was considered adequate for most purposes. Not everyone was fooled by this kind of fraud but many white South Africans, who should have known better, certainly were.

In general, the council concerned itself with matters such as the maintenance of good medical standards within the country and the protection of certain rights claimed by general practitioners. It was also a function of the body to uphold and, if necessary, enforce ethical standards in the medical and dental professions. The council dealt with serious complaints such as accusations of malpractice, inappropriate sexual impropriety or assault that might be made against any medical practitioner. The council would investigate and examine all such complaints and decide whether a doctor's behaviour was sufficiently unprofessional to merit further consideration by a disciplinary sub-committee. The accused, as he then was, would appear before these colleagues with legal representation and, if considered guilty of disgraceful conduct, could be suspended from medical practice for various periods with sentences ranging in severity from a few months cancellation of the right to practice for life.

This system operated in a common-sense way with most permanent suspensions limited to doctors who were clearly, for one reason or another, no longer fit to practice. Dishonesty, the conduct of illegal abortions and adulterous frolics with patients generally attracted a sentence of between 6 and 24 months during which the culprit could not work as a medical practitioner. Peccadilloes that did not involve patients, students or the practice of medicine *per se* did not usually attract the wrath of the council.

On one occasion, a gay, senior, member of the profession made the mistake of bothering a well-built young fellow who was busy relieving himself at a urinal in the public lavatory of a suburban railway station near Cape Town. Unfortunately for the hopeful professor, his quarry was a police sergeant in casual undress. Our hero was immediately arrested and carted off to the local charge-office. Whilst awaiting interview and possible formal arrest he panicked and absconded by jumping through an open ground-floor window. In due course he was charged and released with a warning to behave more circumspectly in future. When a complaint was lodged with the medical council the matter was taken no further on the grounds that the infraction had nothing to do with the ethics or practice of medicine. Possibly his behaviour might earn him some sort of award in the New Year Honours List these days; for the furtherance of minority rights perhaps.

A disgraceful event occurred a year or two before I joined the Medical Council.

Steve Biko was an outspoken black activist whom I had taught and spoken to at some length at the University of Natal Medical School. He was an intelligent man whose ideas, if made public, would have been acceptable to a great many fair-minded members of all the different South African communities. Biko was the kind of man who would be prepared to look for workable compromises. His very existence was, however, like sand between the teeth of the right wing of the

Nationalist government. He was arrested from time to time on the basis of technical infringements and interviewed, which is to say beaten up, by the security police when the mood to do so was upon them.

On the occasion of his final arrest, Biko was severely assaulted by his special branch captors and left unconscious in his cell. Doctors employed by the state, two so-called District Surgeons, examined him and falsely recorded that the prisoner ("detainee" being the euphemism used) had been injured by some unidentified external force. What that might possibly have been, other than a serious assault by his brutish special-branch tormentors was not stated. At the insistence of two of these Neanderthal police, Steve Biko was certified by the doctors as fit to travel some hundreds of miles overland for specialised medical treatment. He was placed in an ambulance without proper supervision and, in transit or shortly after arrival at the chosen destination, died.

There were always at least two threads to the Biko story, although it is unclear that this was appreciated at the time by the responsible authorities. Firstly, there was quite clearly the question of police brutality *per se*. How should it be dealt with and, more importantly, prevented and indeed punished? There has been a great deal written on this topic in recent years and I do not feel qualified to add to a debate which has become dominated by political point scoring between incompatible forces. Suffice it to say that there was just as much whitewash available to the South African government then as there appears to have been to British authorities when they were directed by Edward Heath, the charmless Prime Minister and former Oxford music scholar, to cover up the murderous actions of their uniformed representatives in Derry on Bloody Sunday.

The second thread led one straight to the Medical Council. The doctors involved in the case, who were most certainly intimidated by the police, had falsified documents that required the signature of a registered medical practitioner. By failing to do their duty they effectively delayed the emergency treatment of an individual who was their responsibility. His status as a prisoner made Biko their patient from the moment they first examined him as District Surgeons. Therefore, irrespective of their personal views, attending to his appropriate medical management was their first duty. Without any question these doctors were guilty of thoroughly unprofessional conduct, whether they were threatened by the security police or not. The Medical Council should clearly have disciplined them almost immediately.

It appears that the Minister of Health, to whom the Medical Council was answerable, met with the chairman of council and told him to see to it that the matter of the so-called "Biko Doctors" was not "interfered with" by the Medical Council. Since the majority of council members were sympathetic to the Nationalist party, this proved relatively easy to arrange although a number of members, including those representing the English-language medical schools, objected and raised points of order on several occasions without success. This was a clear case of dereliction of duty and disgraceful conduct on the part of the Biko Doctors as well as by those members of council that followed the ministerial line. Stupidly, all such issues were ignored in the naïve belief by the government and its lap-dogs that the entire affair could be swept under the carpet.

The matter was raised again some years later when I was a member of council and the Surgeon General (who represented the Armed Forces of South Africa) arose during debate to say that the matter should not be discussed since it was essential that the Council should unquestioningly support the police and the national government. A natural autocrat, he sang straight from a Nazi or Communist songbook. Quite how his viewpoint aligned with the moral duties of Council was not apparent.

Times had changed however and a new chairman was in place; a noble and decent Afrikaner, Professor Geldenhuys was somewhat more obedient to his conscience than to Caesar. A majority of council members, including many faithful nationalists, ignored the implied threats of the Surgeon General and voted in favour of investigating the matter as a routine issue of disgraceful conduct.

In due course the two Biko Doctors appeared before a disciplinary sub-committee and their names were removed from the register of medical practitioners. It would be no more than guesswork to suggest what their fate might have been had they done their duty in the first place and defied the security police. No murder charges were ever laid against the men responsible for killing Biko who, naturally enough, became regarded as something of a martyr to his cause. His death was a dreadful waste of a capable man who had more to offer the country than the corrupt, nepotistic, kleptocratic and incompetent governments that emerged much later during the Zuma and Ramaphosa eras.

Other interactions with establishment Afrikaners also taught me that there were tensions present beneath the apparently smooth surface of their society. Here was a white African tribe that had survived the British conquest, lived through the Great Depression and, in finally regaining control of the beloved country, inherited more than gold and diamond mines or wine farms. The bulk of South Africa's population was made up of poorly educated, sometimes atavistic, black Africans. Most Afrikaners were, at that time, well-meaning Christians who were ambivalent about their situation. How to avert the threat to their own nation whilst dealing fairly with the others? Was power-sharing a viable option? At this remove, we now know that the problem was close to insoluble.

One of the areas in which the Nationalist government took an active interest was education. Originally, universities were set up by English-speaking people, soon followed by others who taught in Afrikaans. Initially, talented people who were not white could be admitted to these institutions although there was also an exclusively black university college at Fort Hare, attended *inter alia* by some of the most eminent early leaders of post-colonial southern Africa. Under the Nationalists, separate universities were set up for most, if not all, people classified as "non-white". The standards varied at these "tribal universities" and the lecturers and professors, whilst not uniformly adequate, often included very capable people of all races. Many of them were devoted to the idea of equipping their students to compete with first-world standards, whether at home or abroad. Today that would be mocked as "Eurocentric", at least by those who do not seem to realise how far European standards have fallen.

Whilst serving on the medical Council, an invitation was received to take up the post of Vice-Chancellor at a large medical school, styled the Medical University of South Africa, that had been set up by the government specifically to train black doctors and para-medics, for whom opportunities elsewhere in the country were limited to perhaps 30 or 40 black medical students per year. Like me, the retiring principal was an Oxford graduate but he had been closely associated with the Afrikaner Nationalists.

This seemed a worthwhile project and preliminary enquiries had indicated that important figures in international medicine, who were amongst my personal friends, were willing to act as visiting professors from time to time, thereby helping to improve the profile of the institution, act as role models and keep the standards of tuition at acceptable levels.

Prior to accepting the post, a concerned individual gave me written evidence that a doctrinaire secret society, the Afrikaner Broederbond, had a very real presence amongst the staff of the new university and made it their business to see that government policies were strictly adhered to. This was disturbing enough news but a week or two later my interview with the responsible cabinet minister, in Pretoria, caused me to withdraw my candidature. The man concerned was affable enough and seemed pleased, if not necessarily impressed, that we could converse in Afrikaans. The moment of decision came towards the end of the interview when it became obvious that he had far more interest in whether riot police would be on call to quell any instances of student disobedience than in how academic standards might best be uplifted. In the end, a rather poorly qualified Afrikaner dental practitioner was appointed principal. The stress inherent in the position was such that he suffered a severe cardiovascular collapse a few years after his appointment.

In retrospect, one wonders how that friendly cabinet minister would have responded to the disgraceful, ignorant and moronic behavior of students on campuses in Britain and the United States of America some forty years later. Perhaps every Vice-chancellor should have a hotline to the nearest Flying Squad after all.

THE THRUST COMPANY

One of the major financial successes of the apartheid era in South Africa was a company set up by a very able Afrikaner in order to provide his compatriots with an alternative to the traditional, well established "English" banking, investment and insurance concerns. The founder of this enterprise, a brave, intelligent and highly motivated individual, doubtless had the same drive for success as any other celebrated entrepreneur. It therefore seems reasonable to refer to his great Afrikaner venture as the Thrust Company in recognition of his drive and also of an amusing aspect of certain off-duty activities at management level.

Thrust Co was initially built upon the slightly shaky foundation of contracting poorly secured mortgages and personal loans with people who might have few assets but were considered trustworthy and willing to pay the high interest rates involved. Savings accounts were also on offer and the many appeals made to the public to invest in a truly indigenous project bore fruit. Like similar enterprises of the time, the legal network of the Afrikaner Broederbond (a sort of non-violent *mafia*) and the Reform Churches encouraged their members to move their custom to this new, culturally sympathetic, institution. The company prospered and began to sponsor sporting and social events and, in a number of ways, to entertain some important clients quite royally. *Inter alia,* they were invited to enjoy themselves along lines that at least one member of a European royal family might recognise.

Harold Welsh, known as Cas because he was relaxed and casual, was an older friend who had been involved, as an 18 year-old, in dropping food supplies from an airforce bomber to besieged civilians in Poland. He was a man who considered his words carefully. Cas was measured, deliberate and accurate. After the war he became a surveyor and, in due course, one of three directors of a company with offices on the eighth floor of a building (A) in the centre of Durban, Natal. The main elevator in A was situated within the outside, north-facing, wall of the building and staff members could look out through large windows on either side of the elevator shaft when waiting for the lift to arrive. The windows, always kept clean, afforded a clear view of people moving about a few stories below in the building opposite (B). B was perhaps no more than 35 paces away as the Indian Mynah flies. The Thrust Company had some offices and, in particular, a private suite of reception rooms in B that could easily be spied upon from above by any interested observers who might be waiting beside the closed lift doors in building A.

It was whilst standing there and gazing idly at the buildings outside that Harold noticed lively activity below through the undraped windows of the Thrust Company reception rooms. Not to overstate the case more than necessary, it became obvious to him, after some minutes, that a lunchtime meeting of some sort was in progress and that it involved naturists or perhaps members of some exotic sect with a strange dress-code. At first, he wondered if the people he could see were trying to cope with the oppressive humidity of summer, given that two quite naked young women were standing, drinks in hand, talking to 3 men of a mature age who had discarded all but their undershorts. In the room adjacent he spotted a man he recognised, by his greying hair and handlebar moustache, as Piet van Breda, a senior manager and public relations pundit at the Thrust Company. He, poor fellow, must have been overcome by the heat of the day since he stood beside a rumpled bed, goggle-eyed and gazing at the ceiling, whilst receiving some sort of attention from a third lady of about 20 who was kneeling before him with her back to the window so that no more than her head and bare shoulders were visible from above. Since there was no sign of either the man's shirt or his shorts, both of which had been discarded, Harold wondered, given the sub-tropical heat, if he might be preparing for a tepid-sponging in order to reduce his body temperature.

Of course it soon became evident, even to the naïve and wholesome Harold that the events he was witness to would be considered by most people as far from innocent. Indeed what he saw might even be described as an orgy.

Harold mentioned all this to his colleagues in the office and, in time, a small audience would gather near the lift door each day to enjoy the spectacle below. Several of the players were recognised by the audience and it became clear that this fairly regular sport was sponsored in some way by Thrust Co, providing a sort of bonus to its wealthier, mature, clients. Or was it more like a discount? The complaisant young ladies were staff members, normally serving at counters but now doubtless well on the road to promotion or even marriage to a wealthy oldster. Mr. van Breda acted both as entertainments manager and as an enthusiastic participant.

Sadly, as history teaches us, the temptation to behave in a debauched manner is difficult to resist even amongst the great and the good. This is particularly the case whenever hormonal drives and the prospect of material gains meet one another. For all one knows, the efforts of Piet van Breda might well have been appreciated both by his guests and by the girls who were on the receiving end at the Thrust Co luncheons and all of them would no doubt be indignant if accused of behaving corruptly. Alas! Such is the human condition, it seems.

One man who was highly impressed by the hyperactive Mr. van Breda was the elderly Zulu messenger employed in Harold's office. John Sipho Mdolo was known to have at least 3 wives at home in KwaZulu and was considered to be somewhere between 70 and 80 years old, given the events in Natal's colonial history that he recalled reasonably clearly. It seems likely that John Mdolo saw the efforts of Piet van Breda as impressive rather than comical and, given his domestic arrangements and advancing years, also viewed them with a modicum of envy. The old man approached kindly Harold in confidence to ask if he could find him a supply of the medication the "white boss" with the red hair and moustache was surely taking. Whether or not John Mdolo received a helpful response is not recorded.

In those days, there was not a great deal of social welfare available to anyone other than that provided through a number of charitable organisations. It was therefore hardly surprising that most rural Zulus would look to their own families for support in the long run. Children were, *inter alia,* an insurance against extreme poverty in old age and so it was that fertility in women and potency in men were much admired. The problems associated with feeding and educating a large family that were the inevitable consequence of fecundity were an entirely different matter.

The central position occupied by reproduction in the minds of traditional Zulus was of very great importance to them and could lead to irrational behaviour. What might now be termed conspiracy theories spread quite easily and spells, evil spirits, vaccination, white-man's medicines and something indefinable done by the government were all blamed from time to time as the causes of impotence or infertility. Some even believed that they would be poisoned if they entered a hospital, preferring to take their chances with their own herbalists. In spite of these attitudes, overt displays of sexual incontinence on the part of white people would often lead to polite questions from those Zulus who thought they could possibly gain an edge in their private lives by learning from and emulating the whites in question.

At roughly the same time as the Thrust Co public relations scheme, it was the norm for newspapers to provide information from the courts that dealt with divorce cases. The relevant laws of the time were considerably more involved than they are now and a woman would need to go into great and sometimes intimate detail concerning her marriage if she wished the court to make a sympathetic finding in her favour, Very dirty washing was aired in some cases and the Sunday papers, in particular, took great delight in providing fulsome accounts of the evidence presented. No matter how lurid the details were that were heard by learned judges, newspapers published almost all of them, without fearing any contempt of court proceedings. Of course carefully chosen weasel-words would reflect the *faux* outrage of the journalists.

In one such case, which illustrates the Zulu view mentioned above, a young woman was granted a divorce on grounds of the cruel and unreasonable behaviour of her husband, a city pharmacist who had the general appearance, slender physique (and clearly the stamina) of a stoat or meerkat. The court's ruling followed days of argument during which the plaintiff alleged that, during some ten years of marriage, her husband had habitually demanded his conjugal rights more than twenty times each week and, if not satisfied, would proceed to exercise such rights on his own. She was granted a divorce on grounds, it appeared, of "mental cruelty" which neatly avoided any mention of satyriasis (or nymphs). There was much tut-tutting on the part of the great and the good in the white community but the pharmacist's business absolutely thrived, doubling its turnover within days of the case being published. Zulu males came in droves to purchase the vitamins that our hero wisely recommended. Of course, these pills would have a decent placebo effect and gave rise, if those words are appropriate, to a satisfactory response in perhaps thirty-percent of customers. This response was enough to keep his business, like himself, in robust good health.

Naturally enough, the fertility rate of the Zulus and other black groups did not go unnoticed by the white government of the day. It required no great intelligence to work out that black Africans would eventually swamp other cultures and inherit the country, for better or worse.

In an attempt to delay the inevitable, the government began a programme of propaganda urging white families to be "fruitful and multiply". This is an official approach that has never been needed peasant populations, whether in Zululand, South Asia, Brasil or Connemara. As it happened, whites who still thought in the old rural way were in short supply and, instead of taking the matter seriously, made a joke of it. The South African cabinet minister who had called on every white family to have a child at that particular time was voted, in a poll conducted by a newspaper, as "National Sportsman of the Year". Like many South African politicians of the day, his surname was Botha.

AMADODA, ABAFAZI.

My first introduction to a person of any race or ethnic group other than my own happened well before I was able to walk. During the war years, from 1939 to 1945, my father was "up north", with the South African Second and Sixth Divisions facing up to the enemy in Libya, Egypt and Italy. My mother and grandmother were left to cope, as best they could, with domestic affairs. Four of us, including myself and Mick, my older brother, lived with our pet cat in a small house at 19, Milner Street, Grahamstown.

Mother and Gran were supported by the largely good-natured efforts of two, Xhosa-speaking, women (*abafazi*) who shared the household duties and kept an eye on the two small boys. The cook and nanny were related to one another by marriage and stayed in properly constructed outbuildings in the back yard, perhaps 30 paces from the kitchen door. After the fashion of most normal children, we did not really register that these happy, uncomplicated people were of a different shape or colour to ourselves or that they spoke to each other in a strange language full of difficult click-sounds. We were mostly impressed by the facts that they spoke loudly, laughed a lot and sometimes conducted long, animated conversations with friends who might be two or three-hundred yards distant. It seemed unfair that we had to act more modestly and never to shout except at rugby matches. Their food, a mixture of maize and beans cooked on the kitchen stove, interested us mainly because we were not allowed to taste it. We wondered why they were permitted to wash themselves in a zinc bath out in the sunshine with water from the garden tap, sometimes warmed in a kettle, whereas we had to rely upon a rickety old wood and pine-cone-burning geyser to heat our bathwater indoors.

The terminology in use at the time was strangely Victorian (perhaps with its roots in colonialism), although it did not seem odd to toddlers who knew nothing else. In our home it was customary for the cook and general helper, a mature and strapping woman of at least 60, and hew younger assistant, our nanny, to be spoken of as "the girls". Not in the pathetic American sense of 90-year-old "girls" all together in an expensive restaurant but in a way that was slightly dismissive; as in "servant girls". Many of the rural African women employed in the homes of whites at that time had attended mission schools for short periods and had been given Christian names that the English tongue, whether forked or furry, could get around. Hence the many whites who, years later, still remembered their kindly and patient nannies, numbers of *abafazi* with names like Beatrice, Gertrude, Mavis and Winifred.

If this was patronising, it was not entirely so. There also existed an undercurrent of envy on the part of the whites for the simple life that was still led by many of the rural AmaXhosa in those days. When my father returned home after the war, his bedtime stories mostly concerned the adventures of an imaginary Xhosa boy of our age named Donsiwe. A few of our wider family were expert linguists and one, my great uncle, Archdeacon Walter Leary, was a renowned Mpondophile who translated biblical texts into the vernacular. Though this might well be regarded as dastardly by current left-wing opinion-leaders and atheists, he was filled with love and respect for his friends and fellow pilgrims, whatever their race or background.

In my case, after the age of about 7, contact with black Africans was very limited until I entered medical school and learned, to my surprise, that by no means all of them were from the Xhosa or Zulu-speaking septs. Witwatersrand University provided an environment in which the prospect of an end to segregation and the possible consequences of such a change were frequently and openly discussed. It was clear, even to the politically naive, that the apartheid system of those days was woefully unfair. However there was much difference of opinion over whether or not a majority black government would make matters worse. Basically, nearly all my fellow students wanted to see the lives of blacks improved and some sort of equal opportunity system introduced with the preservation of decent, civilized, standards. Alas for the idealism and good intentions of the young! Freedom came in due course followed, a dozen or so years thereafter, by chaos.

In the course of the decades that followed I worked in hospitals that catered for Zulu patients, taught African students and interacted with the black men (*amadoda*) and women (*abafazi*) who worked with me. They are remembered for a variety of reasons but one of the most interesting and striking features of their behaviour, in many but not all cases, was their reluctance to abandon many of the old traditions of African culture in spite of domination by powerful forces from both the west and the east. This had the virtue of preserving some things that were beautiful but, unfortunately, also had some miserable consequences.

A typical example of the latter came to light at the Natal University Medical School when I worked there. A detailed research project by paediatricians and pathologists was able to prove that previously unexplained deaths in Zulu infants were caused by liver failure following the administration of traditional enemas. These were prepared from an indigenous plant belonging to the daisy family. The news was, of course, received with total disbelief by most of the tribal herbalists and also by their disciples. Certainly the world view of the average rural Zulu or Xhosa was, and perhaps remains, far removed from that of most educated individuals today. To them, the strangers that settled in their territory were just that-strange. They preferred their own ways. Even so, most white South Africans were grievously at fault and deserved criticism for showing little or no interest in the fascinating cultural history and beautiful, expressive, languages of their black countrymen.

As a doctor with some interest in the Zulu predicament of the time, it was not unheard of for neighbours to bring their ill or injured staff to me for attention. In the next door house but one, a black man named

JUST BEFORE DARK

Enoch Makhatini was employed as gardener and general labourer. He was a small, wiry and prodigiously strong Zulu of about 40 with an almost unquenchable thirst for the illicit, highly toxic, liquor brewed in servants' quarters by women down our street. Enoch's origins were uncertain, though Reginah Shange, our own, much loved, domestic worker, hinted darkly at a history of expulsion from a tribal group living in a place to the north of Zululand known as the Makhatini flats. He was a sort of Zulu exile or asylum-seeker though without any remittance from a welfare system or support from Hampstead liberals.

In spite of, or perhaps because of, his stoat-like physique Enoch, or Makhatini as he was usually addressed, had the reputation of being a latter-day Casanova. His interactions with women and alcohol usually were involved when my medical intervention on his behalf was called for.

The signal that indicated Enoch needed assistance was usually not his employer at my front door but the sound of raucous singing coming from the road outside our family home in the middle of the night. Most of the time Makhatini would be found lying on the grass verge, oblivious to his surroundings and giving vent to some half-remembered Shembe hymn or other. His employer would be summoned and, having established that he was uninjured, two of us would carry the feisty little man to his bed. His extraordinary strength and apparent indifference to the later symptoms of alcohol poisoning were such that Enoch would consistently be out mowing the lawn in the humid summer conditions no later than 9 a.m. the next day. He seemed to be as contented as any *isibankwa* (lizard) in the sunshine.

On two occasions worth recalling Enoch Makhatini did not get away with his spree drinking quite so lightly. He had a particularly vivid relationship with a local Zulu woman, one Beauty Mkhize, a renowned brewer of unspeakably foul-smelling alcoholic beverages. On more than one occasion, she took a dim view of his casual attitude to sexual fidelity and decided to teach him a lesson. One evening, when he was helplessly drunk, she beat him comprehensively about the head with a large glass bottle she had first filled with tap-water to lend more weight and meaning to her assault. To hazard a guess as to the thickness of Enoch's skull would be to invite abuse from the politically correct quarter but it was frankly astonishing to find, after hearing the story and being summoned to assist, that he was fully conscious, if bleary-eyed. He had suffered no more than a number of minor scalp lacerations that needed stitching together. The bottle, on the other hand, was broken into 3 pieces.

On a later occasion Makhatini was brought to my door with the complaint that his principal *inamorata*, Beauty the talented brewer, had stabbed him in the chest with a kitchen knife. This time, her efforts to discipline him had more serious consequences than usual in that she had punctured a lung in her frenzy. The left upper quadrant of his chest felt like a sheet of bubble-wrap paper, the air having infiltrated the tissues between lung and skin, producing crepitations or popping sounds if pressed upon. After xrays had been examined, a suitable drain was inserted in his chest and Enoch returned to his duties in 5 days. No charges were laid.

To everyone's amazement, Enoch Makhatini lived for more than 20 years after these adventures, successfully dodging both the HIV microorganism and the violence of his lady friends. He reached a good age and died with his liver the consistency of a Zulu brave's ox-hide shield thanks to long hours spent down the years, relaxing in various shebeens soaking up liters of witches brew.

One of the *amadoda* with diametrically opposed habits to Enoch the gardener came to my attention at roughly the same time.

Bongani Mayosi was an exceptionally talented and charming man of the kind that the world simply does not seem able to recognize and embrace at the right time. In a sense he was to African medicine what Vincent van Gogh was to art; his gifts and their potential value to mankind appreciated rather too late in the day.

Bongani, the son of a doctor based in the Xhosa heartlands, came to

Natal to study medicine. In the mid-1980s he spent a year in the Clinical Pharmacology department as a sort of sabbatical from his clinical studies and obtained a bachelor's degree in medical science. He simply sailed through the course before going on to qualify as a medical doctor, with multiple distinctions, a year or so later.

Dr Mayosi went from strength to strength when he left Natal and was soon widely recognised as a world-class researcher in several fields but most notably that of cardiology. Numerous awards came his way, not least an Oxford doctorate, and he was appointed Professor of Medicine at the University of Cape Town at a young age and definitely upon merit alone. So, to an extent, he was already faring rather better than poor van Gogh who sold only a single painting during his lifetime. From time to time news of him came my way or we would bump into each other at a medical conference somewhere in Europe. His productivity and the international recognition he rightly earned were astonishing. Just a Xhosa boy from Mthatha he might have said.

Bongani's reputation and ability were such that he was later installed as Dean of the Faculty of Medicine at Cape Town. No doubt he accepted the post because of his well-developed sense of duty and because he believed he could help greatly to support the cause of talented students from all backgrounds whatever their colour or provenance. It proved to be a fatal mistake.

At around the time of his appointment, the woeful African National Congress had started to interfere directly in the affairs of previously independent universities. *Inter alia* the half-witted woke idea that anyone who registered as a student merited a degree, regardless of performance, was actively supported by ignorant government propagandists. Student agitators took advantage of the climate that this idiocy created and demanded that tuition fees be reduced or done away with altogether. To emphasise their case, as has been typical of "mass action" worldwide, students intimidated staff, boycotted lectures and burned down campus buildings when they could. Facilities such as libraries and administrative buildings were favourite targets.

Professor Mayosi, one suspects, found himself in an impossible situation. As an African, he surely had some sympathy for the struggling student body not all of whom shared his great intellectual gifts or relatively comfortable family background. He would have been under pressure from the usual dim politicians to lower academic standards, or perhaps admit the occasional retarded relative to the university. He would have resisted academic corruption in the face of bare-faced intimidation. A First World man he was caught in a Third World scenario and would have been unable to give adequate attention to his own important African and international research projects. The university, or so it has been said, left him isolated and unsupported.

A better man than most of us, Bongani despaired and took his own life, aged 51.

We still speak of "Greek Tragedies". The generic term should rather be "Human Tragedies". The story of Bongani Mawethu Mayosi is one such.

NEIGHBOURS

Our home in Natal was furnished after the style of the day; comfortable chairs, built-in wardrobes, rosewood tables, woollen carpets and framed prints of paintings by old masters on the walls. Nothing was unconventional or unusual, except for one very old and battered-looking bookshelf. This had been handmade by someone living on the eastern frontier of the Cape Colony during the mid-19th century, using primitive tools and timber cut from a great South African yellow-wood tree. It had once belonged to my Irish great-grandfather.

William Leary came to Africa as a drummer-boy with the 75th Regiment of Foot in 1837, later trading in British Kaffraria, an area north of the Great Fish River to the east of South Africa. It was then, and still remains, the home of the isiXhosa-speaking peoples; Mpondo, Mpondomise and Tembu amongst many others. At sunset William, who had been schooled as a boy by the Anglican Vicar of Naas in County Kildare, would assemble his family and house servants in the parlour, take his bible from the yellow-wood bookcase, and lead a brief act of worship.

Life on the frontier was not entirely without its stresses and neighbours of vastly different cultures were unlikely to be on good terms at all times. It is perhaps worth mentioning that when the Nguni tribes first moved into the Cape, six or seven centuries ago, the indigenous San people referred to them as *Xhosa* which in their language of many click-sounds means *the angry people*.

The Leary trading-post and home were burnt to the ground by marauders during the long-forgotten Mpondomise rebellion of 1880. Nothing escaped the blaze except the handmade bookcase which was taken from the house by a loyal servant and hidden somewhere amongst the prickly-pears and thorn-bushes of the veld. It was retrieved some months later, slightly scarred by fire in one place but otherwise none-the-worse for its exposure to sun, rain, wind and wild animals. It still serves its purpose today, thousands of miles away from southern Africa, in my County Waterford home.

A few hours before the destruction of his property William had loaded his wife, daughters and younger sons onto an ox-wagon and set out, on an unmade road and across the wilds, to escape the violence and take refuge in a neighbouring small town. He was unarmed except for his hunting rifle and it is unlikely that anyone in the small party was distracted by the many potholes on the way.

The Leary group must have presented a tempting target to the insurgents who were preparing to ambush them in the hills a few miles along the track. Whatever the rebels had in mind, it should be recorded that even though most Xhosa tribesmen were savage and merciless in battle, they also had a strict and quite admirable code of honour modern warlords might do well to imitate. They seldom, if ever, attacked women and children, preferring to release them when besieging a place before getting down to the more important and pleasant business of butchering the men.

Just as the wagon reached the shallow gorge where the Mpondomise were hiding, a mighty electrical storm broke out. There was a loud clap of thunder immediately overhead and a lightning bolt struck the stony track just ahead of the paired oxen, running along the chain between them. How this failed to kill any of the animals or people on the wagon is something of a mystery. William's rifle was buckled by the blast and rendered useless.

The men waiting by the chosen ambush-site witnessed all of this and fled from the scene at great speed, shouting to one another that Tixo, Almighty God, had intervened on behalf of the white people. Quite so, even if sudden thunderstorms are common enough in subtropical Africa. As with most miracles, timing is everything.

The Leary party, complete with decommissioned rifle, continued on its way and safely reached the fortified government buildings at their destination. There they remained for several days with other colonists, under siege, until the rebellion was put down by the local reservists, two of whom were William Leary's sons; my schoolboy grandfather (described at the time as "a fearless boy" and "crack shot") and his older brother, William Power Leary. It has never been a good idea to irritate the Irish.

Naturally enough, South Africa changed between 1880 and the late 20th century as a result of commerce, education and the development of its infrastructure. In some respects, things stayed the same. Where wildlife existed, the old pleasures and hazards of game viewing and hunting remained and, in rural areas especially, most of the ancient tribal customs and beliefs survived amongst the black peoples.

Far from the influences of Europe, Arabia and Asia, Africans were at a disadvantage. The world view of a rural Xhosa or Zulu youngster, given little schooling and exposed from infancy to the age-old, established traditions and beliefs of his people, was unlikely ever to be identical to that of a privileged white individual of the same age. Not a question of intelligence but one of different cultural approaches and opportunities. Understanding one another was never easy. We saw the world from different perspectives and yet some room could be found for friendship and mutual help. The background noise of the old struggle between races was always with us.

One of our neighbours, Rupert Fingleton, was a man of many skills. He repaired, refitted and assembled broken things for his clients, banging away in his repair-shop with the help of his black assistant, a Mr. D. H. Dlamini. They had worked together productively and in mutual respect for a dozen years or more when disorder in the tribal areas outside Durban threatened to disrupt their little business.

Political agitators had dictated that no one was to leave the local villages to work for white people and, always as happy to resort to violence as any half-witted campus "demonstrator", had begun to burn down the houses of anyone who did not join the strike. Traitors to the cause were likely to be killed out of hand if at home when the extremists made their midnight calls although, mercifully, the day of the unspeakably cruel and wicked "necklacing" executions, supported by the psychopathic Winnie Mandela, had not yet arrived. The government of the day was cynically unperturbed by what was taking place, quite content that the Zulus were kept preoccupied by problems that were restricted to rural areas. If the authorities intervened at all, it was a muted response that they made.

Somehow, D.H., as he was always called, managed to remain as even-tempered and reliable as ever, reporting for work promptly each morning, albeit looking slightly rumpled, muddy and tired. When Fingleton complimented him on his loyalty and determination and asked how long he thought he could avoid being murdered in his own home, D.H. replied that there was nothing to worry about. "No sir", he said, "I burned down my own house last week and now I sleep in the bushes, so I am safe". Until other arrangements could be made, a cot was provided for him in the Fingleton garage.

In spite of differences in world-view there were considerable interactions between the races since, hatred, mindless violence and corruption notwithstanding, rich veins of humanity, decency and kindness are to be found amongst both white and black Africans. In the South, caring for others is known as *Ubuntu* and unquestioning loyalty and affection between black and white existed to a significant extent for many years before the happy, if brief, public reconciliations that attended the appearances on the scene of great men such as Nelson Mandela and Desmond Tutu.

Long before the concept of *Ubuntu* was explained to the white community, evidence of mutual respect could be found, at least anecdotally. One great uncle of my Irish line retired from his post as a country magistrate to live in a small Eastern Cape market-town, not far from the tumbledown villages of Xhosa people. One morning he was sitting in his front garden drinking tea with a spoonful of whiskey when he was greeted by a black, middle-aged, passer-by. A conversation in isiXhosa followed, during which the stranger volunteered that, as he was a poor man, he would be obliged if the white man would give him a live rooster and two hens from amongst his large brood of chickens. This, he said, would be on "traditional terms". Feeling sorry for the man and clearly having fowls to spare, my uncle gave the man three of his best birds and, sending him on his way, forgot the incident completely.

Five years later, frail by now, the old man was called to the front of the house by the daughter who lived with him. Standing by the gate with three fine cows was the stranger to whom he had once given three chickens. The man courteously explained that, in accordance with the Xhosa custom, he was bound to repay the debt he owed plus interest. He had used the gift wisely, selling eggs and breeding birds for the table. He was now a wealthy man, by tribal standards, and the owner of many cattle. The pick of his herd stood at the gate in payment of his debt.

At his age, the white man could not manage the "interest" that had accrued on his investment of three fowls. So he thanked the Xhosa debtor, shook his hand and asked him to give the cattle to one of his own, preferably a poor man. So Uncle Bill's original modest gift came eventually to benefit a third family and perhaps others in time.

There was another illustration of *Ubuntu* or certainly of unashamed compassion and brotherhood between men of different races at the funeral of my 93 year old friend Eduoard Andries some years ago. A decent and harmless individual who boasted that he had been conceived in Paris, Eddie had lived quietly and simply all his life, helping the poor of all races and obeying Christ's commandment that we should love others as ourselves. Kindly and defenceless Eddie was shot dead one night in his home by a young Zulu burglar. It seems that he panicked when the old man awoke and challenged him.

A week later, at the funeral, the saddest mourner, other than Eddie's widow, was Absalom Mkhize, an octogenarian Zulu cook and general factotum, who had worked for the family for four or five decades. The white-haired old fellow acted as chief pallbearer, helping to carry the coffin of his friend and master to its resting place with tears of grief streaming down his cheeks. After the ceremony, the dear man was no longer just another black servant. He was surrounded by concerned white people, men and women, embracing him, wiping tears from their own eyes and trying to comfort him. This was an extraordinary illustration of the fact that unconditional love is an infinitely more powerful force for good than is hatred. What a shame that this truth, known for millennia, has been largely ignored almost ever since, most notably by politicians and chancers motivated by their own greed.

REGINAH SHANGE

Reginah Shange was an utterly good, kindly and loyal woman who worked as our domestic helper in Natal half a century ago. She was not quite literate even in her own language but learned to communicate with us in English quite well after a year or two. From a tribal area about 25 miles from our home, she lived in a hut with her 2 children who had been sired by a sometime taxi-driver who seldom put in an appearance and paid nothing towards their upkeep. He had at least 3 other, more important, fertile wives and expected Reginah to be self-supporting. Like many African women, she was a loving, naturally protective, mother and treated my two little girls and their older brother with great tenderness and patience. To our shame, we never mastered the intricacies of her people's beautiful and expressive isiZulu and could only communicate using short phrases; rather like a moronic leftwing "student" at a demonstration. At least we never learnt the Zulu for "from the river to the sea".

During weekdays Reginah lived in a room, with adjacent shower and lavatory just beyond the kitchen door. It was always kept spotlessly clean and tidy. The brass bed, faithful to the customs of the Nguni peoples of southern Africa, was supported at its four corners by two or three bricks propping up each leg to raise the bed another 8 or 12 inches above the floor. This ruse, it was generally believed, would frustrate the attempts of Tokoloshe, (a diminutive, ancient and malignant goblin and would-be incubus), to climb into the bed whilst its occupant slept. It must have worked quite well most of the time, given that over the dozen or more years she was with us her room only needed the attentions of an exorcising priest on one occasion.

One morning, when all the family were out for a few hours, a young black man, of dubious intent, tried to climb over the high garden wall with a cocked and loaded revolver in one hand. Slipping, he took a bullet to the head, killing himself. This was witnessed through the kitchen window by a terrified Reginah, who ran across to the neighbours for assistance. By the time the police arrived to investigate, an army of large flies were tucking into the spilt blood and one or two of them had come into the kitchen through an open window, it being a hot and sunny day. Reginah, who had been recovering her equanimity with a cup of sweet tea witnessed the arrival of the bloodied flies and became very upset. According to some Zulu, and probably a few other, traditions the presence of a dead man's blood in the house meant that his spook, or ghost, might haunt the premises for years to come. No more than an interesting superstition, we thought but Reginah found it convincing enough.

Comfort was provided by the local vicar, who understood Zulu folklore, and came to the house, suitably attired, to conduct an act of exorcism. After a brief ceremony complete with candles and bells, everyone was able to carry on as before. It is true however that, just in case the *mfundisi* (priest) did not really have any say over the disposal of African spirits, Reginah also took out further insurance by purchasing a few traditional artefacts from her tribal witchdoctor. These were placed strategically, near her door and on the windowsill of her room.

In a year or two, after obtaining permission from her tribal chieftain, we built a small cottage for Reginah out in the beautiful valleys that lie between the two main cities of Natal. She would commute back and forth by bus, spending the weekends with her children and much of the week with us. During a period when I was away attending a conference in Europe, a problem arose. In 1989, whether it was popular or not anywhere else, witchcraft still enjoyed a wide following amongst ordinary Africans. Many Zulus still believed that whatever was experienced in life, whether it brought health, illness, an untimely death, wealth or poverty, harmony or violence, could be accounted for by spirits, demons, curses and magical spells. Plants and animal parts, the rarer the better, played a vital role in both the casting and the breaking of spells.

Reginah came to work as usual one day and announced that the witchdoctors in her district were abducting small children to use for *umuthi*. In simple terms this meant that they were being murdered and their organs harvested for use as components of particularly strong, spell-breaking medicines. Reginah's small boy, Shaka, named for a great Zulu king and despot of the Napoleonic era, was perhaps 6 or 7 years old at the time. A handsome little ebony chap, he would sometimes visit our home with his mother to the delight of my daughters.

Reginah was sent home on the next available bus to fetch Shaka so that he could be kept in safety at our home. The little Zulu boy spent the next few weeks as a member of the Leary household, living in our youngest daughter's room whilst she was away at university and sitting, entranced, in front of the television screen in the sitting-room each evening. He remained happy and spoiled, until the crisis in the hills had been dealt with, somewhat reluctantly, by the white forces of law and order.

There was only one blemish on Reginah's record and that was so slight that no one with a sense of humour would have been offended by it for long. It arose because she, being a devout and God-fearing woman, was unaccustomed to strong drink and, furthermore, was unable to metabolise alcohol at anything like a reasonable rate.

At that time it was usual amongst whites, when entertaining a group of friends at home, to arrange for the domestic helpers to work for a few extra hours on the day in question. They would generally serve the meal, clear the table and wash the dishes and beer and wine glasses whilst the guests were still in the house talking and drinking coffee. Providing these services attracted a bonus of at least a day's wages. Opportunities to work late were much sought after by Reginah, particularly since she was excused from serving breakfast the morning after a late dinner or party. One evening, a party was held in our house in order to celebrate a birthday or some other significant landmark. In view of the amount of work that would be involved, Reginah invited a friend from along the road to assist her, not knowing that she, Rosie Madondo, was more than partial to a sip or three of alcohol now and then.

That evening the guests were offered beer or spirits as an aperitif, followed by a choice of wines deemed complementary to the first, second and third courses, supplemented later by a fine choice of liquers. At regular intervals glasses were collected and taken to the kitchen to be washed. In no time at all Rosie noticed, to her satisfaction, that not all the wine glasses had been fully drained. She saw to it that this state of affairs was promptly rerectified, generously sharing the pickings with Reginah, the uninitiated innocent.

Once the last guest had left, Rosie was paid her dues and was sent on her way home further up the road, singing happily and not bothered if she walked with imperfect coordination. Of Reginah Shange there was no sign at all, either in the house or in her own room.

Not feeling particularly strong and aware of the venomous creatures known to be abroad at dead of night, two of us went somewhat unsteadily into the garden with our torches and began calling her name. After a few minutes we heard a Zulu anthem, coming from the direction of the small indigenous wood that surrounded the more formal, cultivated, part of the garden. Following the sound of her song, we came upon the cheerful form of our beloved Reginah. Still dressed in her best clothes, but by now a trifle dishevelled, she lay on her back amongst the rushes on the fringe of a small pond, otherwise the natural retreat of frogs, water-snakes, small wading birds and a range of biting insects. Quite oblivious to her surroundings and the spectacle she presented, she seemed in a very expansive mood, singing what sounded like a hymn a little too raucously. Briefly put, she was blind drunk.

Reginah was escorted to her room, given two aspirins, and left overnight to her own devices. Next morning she reported for work, shamefaced and remorseful but well-scrubbed and neatly dressed. She had a small bruise over her left ear, presumably the result of colliding with an overhanging branch in the wood during her escapade of the night before. She soon became her old self again after receiving absolution at our hands, willingly given. Not wishing her to lose face, our amusement remained hidden. It was a more-or-less harmless, and temporary fall from grace. Reginah was a vocal apologist for the tea-total life ever after.

Some years later we left South Africa behind us, selling our home and moving to Ireland. When it was time to go, I witnessed a deeply affecting scene outside our old home. It involved two middle-aged mothers, one white and descended from Celts and Norman English, the other black, a Zulu with ancient ancestry in the forests of Central Africa.

The two women were my wife Patricia, a privileged white South African madam and Reginah Shange, her humble Zulu servant and loyal friend of the past 15 years. They left the house together, embraced and clung to each other, weeping bitterly, whilst the taxi that would take us to the airport waited nearby. I stood within earshot, trying not to be drawn into their distress but biting my lip that would not stop quivering.

"Now you are going, I am never to be happy on the world again!" the Zulu woman said in her best English. Indeed she was right and it was so.

Both women passed on within twenty years of that farewell. Surely they were to meet again beyond the bounds of what we humans know of time, space and matter; perhaps even at Heaven's gate. I believe as much.

EMERSON AND OBED

In the humid climate of Natal, suburban lawns, shrubs and flowers grew almost overnight and there was always work for any of the would-be gardeners who waited to be hired, on a day-to-day basis, at the local labour exchanges. We employed a number of these men over the years, most of whom were willing and friendly though not always able to communicate in English. There were some exceptions to this rule.

One day Emerson Ngidi knocked on our front door looking for work. He was a fine looking young man of about 25 and, as a graduate of a nearby mission school, spoke almost perfect English. His grand-sounding Christian-name had been given to him by the missionaries, which was the norm when African babies were baptised in a Christian church. His real name, given and used by his Zulu parents, was actually Siyabonga, meaning "we praise you" or, roughly, "thanks". It might be worth mentioning that, just as most Zulus were given a biblical first name by the churches without much consultation, white settlers were given Zulu names by the tribesmen. Such nicknames were usually descriptive of the person concerned; not always complimentary but often gentle and affectionate. Thus, a famous good-humoured missionary doctor, with a particularly wild beard, was called *mahleka umhlatini* or "he who laughs in the forest". An elderly neighbour with a very pronounced stoop was known as *kubhekephansi* or "the one who looks at the ground" or "face down". My own Zulu name, perhaps because I was taller than most Zulus, was *hambelaphezulu* or, roughly "walker in the heavens". Certainly grander and more poetic than being called "lofty" or "Johnny head in air".

Emerson was duly hired to work on Tuesdays and Fridays each week during the summer and was soon accepted and trusted by the family, including my wife and the two small girls who used to go out to talk to him in the garden. We were so impressed that after a few weeks I used my official notepaper to write a glowing reference that Emerson could use when looking for work to fill the days of the week when he was not engaged at our home.

Early on a Monday morning some months later, I was called from my study by Reginah Shange who announced that Emerson wished to speak to me. At the front door I found him with a young woman, who was wrapped in a blanket that partly obscured her features and who was rocking to and fro, moaning softly. Her cheeks were tear-stained. Emerson was agitated and held a grubby piece of paper in one hand, an invoice as it turned out.

The young man was clearly very upset and explained that he did not know what to do. Their 2 month old baby had died on Friday night and the little body was being kept at a funeral home near his hut in the valley. They had no money to pay for a coffin or funeral and the undertaker, a Mr Parbhoo, refused to release or bury the child's body until he received a hefty advance payment. He was also charging them a daily "storage rate" until burial took place. In the two days that had passed their debt already amounted to two weeks wages.

As anyone else would, I wrote a cheque to cover all Emerson's expenses and gave it to him. More than a little pompously, I said "Bury your child Ngidi. This money is for you, a present, not a debt to be repaid. Just remember that it was a white man that has looked after you". I suppose that this gesture impressed Emerson for he brought his best friend Obed Sithole to the garden a week or two later so that he could meet this strange member of the oppressing classes.

In those days I was young, arrogant and foolish enough to think that I understood the Zulu people simply because of working amongst them for a few years. Of course this was not so and, in reality, I knew very little. Few people, after all, are able to really grasp all the nuances of a stranger's culture. So it was that the next developments came as a complete surprise to me.

Whilst at work one morning I was telephoned by a well-spoken senior policeman, one Lieutenant Visagie. The letter of recommendation that I had written for Emerson Ngidi had been found at the scene of a serious crime and the police wished to find him. The preliminary evidence indicated that, when not otherwise engaged, Emerson and Obed had robbed some houses, when the occupants were either asleep or absent, and stolen two loaded pistols. They had then amused themselves by testing the firearms, shooting randomly at other black people waiting beside a township bus stop. Several of their innocent targets had died of their wounds.

Whilst I listened to Lt. Visagie's story, our gardener turned gunman was mowing the lawn at my home and my two young daughters were playing there by themselves, it being a school holiday. I telephoned the house at once and told the girls to lock themselves upstairs and await the arrival of the police. Emerson was collected by them in good time and taken away, suitably restrained. He served some 5 years in prison for culpable homicide, the tariff for an offence of this kind being modest during the apartheid years if both perpetrator and victim happened to be black. White on black violence was regarded as even less heinous at that time but a black man who killed a white person could expect to become briefly acquainted with the hangman in Pretoria. Not exactly an even-handed approach.

Shortly after his release from prison on licence Emerson returned to me to ask for his old job, mindful perhaps of the kindness with which he had once been treated. No doubt this was a great compliment but any idea of returning a convicted killer to the family circle, rehabilitated or not, was firmly quashed by my wife and, most adamantly, by Reginah Shange. When I last heard of Emerson, he had joined an athletics club in the city with a view to becoming a distance runner. That was perhaps 45 years ago.

UNSUNG AFFECTION

Some years ago Martyn Lewis, a well-known television journalist, caused a stir by applying Gresham's monetary law to journalism. Whereas Gresham said something to the effect of "bad money drives out good", Lewis observed that bad news drives out good news and that sensationalism drives out balance in media reports. The accuracy of his claim can be judged, in accordance with whatever personal biases are present, by anyone who follows news bulletins broadcast by any number of contemporary television stations.

For decades, liberal journalists took delight in publicising whatever was negative and unjust in the governance of South Africa and Rhodesia by white minorities. In general, unsympathetic, left-wing journalists carefully avoided any mention of the charity, support and compassion shown towards their black countrymen by many members of the white settler communities that lived in, developed and transformed those countries. The same pathetic group of dishonest, malcontents nowadays ignores the wholesale chaos, corruption and incompetence of black governments in the "liberated" countries and appears quite indifferent to the suffering of the black underclass that has resulted from the regime change they were so insistent upon. It needs stating that, just as the old white autocrats were opposed by significant numbers of their own people, on both humanitarian and simple common-sense grounds, many brave, black Africans question and oppose their own racist, self-serving, corrupt politicians today. None more outspoken, in recent times, than the late Christian Archbishop of Cape Town, Desmond Tutu.

The fact of the matter is that even in the midst of the unprecedented violence, graft and incompetence of contemporary

Southern Africa there remains a hard core of people who choose love over hate and reconciliation over resentment and retribution. It was my great good fortune to meet many such people.

It has long been the custom in the English-speaking world for the high-schools and universities, mainly attended by privileged middle-class pupils as they are, to hold reunions at 5 or 10 year intervals. These usually take place on or near the old school premises and, to be cynical, provide an opportunity for the institution to collect donations from its former students. The alumni, or former "learners" as they are now appallingly called, (due, no doubt, to the difficulties that Americans and other poorly educated people have in expressing themselves in plain English), enjoy renewing old friendships and reminiscing. Naturally enough, as the years pass by so the accuracy of what the ageing former "learners" recall diminishes and an interesting range of quite untrue narratives emerges.

Some years ago, I attended just such a reunion at my old school. It was both inconvenient and expensive to stay near the school and so a room, was secured for 3 days in a charming, family run, bed-and-breakfast establishment, near to the seaside and perhaps two hours by road from Cape Town. The resort in question is called Hermanus and there, in season, it is still possible to sit on a terrace above the sea and watch whales amusing themselves in the bay below.

On the first morning of the stay, breakfast was served in the small dining-room by a plump, happy, Xhosa woman of about 50; roughly the same age as my children. As Beatrice Kusasa was particularly talkative, I asked her where she was from (apparently considered a loaded, racist, question by the liberal-left these days) and was delighted to hear that her family home was a small city in the Albany district of the Eastern Cape, namely Grahamstown. "Snap", as the old card game used to have it. Grahamstown (renamed "Makhanda") was the small cathedral city where my grandfather had served as a magistrate, my mother had been a star academic, my father had been a member of the local rugby team and adjutant in the local First City regiment and where

I had been born and spent my very early childhood.

At that stage, breakfast was largely forgotten and the conversation became quite animated. I remembered a few short isiXhosa phrases learnt in my nursery days and Beauty said she thought that we might be related. This comment was made in jest but taken as a compliment. Such a link was of course possible, if remotely so, given that my family's presence in the Albany district went back to 1820. Settlers at that time were not always averse to taking indigenous mistresses, discreetly or otherwise, with the usual consequences. This established, she asked me, with all the innocent curiosity of her kindly background, how old I was. When I told her that my 76th birthday fell two days later she was delighted and told me that, whilst she was not on duty that day, she would bake a birthday cake for me and see that it was delivered to my table by her colleagues.

A chocolate cake, complete with a few lighted candles, was duly presented to me at breakfast 48 hours later by two shy Xhosa waitresses, singing "Happy Birthday to You" with an African beat.

On my last day in Hermanus, before I drove away, Beauty Kusasa, dressed for work in her pinafore and cap, came to say goodbye. She hugged me tightly and said, "We will meet again in the heavens". A comment made by a good and compassionate, woman with affection and sincerity. As fellow Anglicans might put it, I approach that prospect *in sure and certain hope.*

This was no isolated incident and probably anyone whose family has a long association with Africa can tell similar stories. The mutual devotion and loyalty to one another that sometimes develops between people of different ethnicities and with differing world views can be inspirational and moving. It might have been relatively rarely found in the worlds of South African business and industrial affairs but it was clear to see amongst the men and women who chose to work as doctors, nurses and teachers amongst neighbours of other races most in need of their help.

It would be difficult to know whether the more progressive whites of the time were motivated by compassion or by guilt-feelings; at this stage all that matters is that real efforts were made by some to improve the lives of the poor and the wretched. In my own circle, medical students of several universities worked voluntarily as night-school teachers and ran medical clinics in the run-down townships occupied by large numbers of impoverished blacks who had moved to the cities seeking work. At my medical school, senior students spent a two week period working in just such an unpleasant place, attending to sick and sometimes malnourished people at a central clinic building or in their own miserable shacks. Of course, such privation is intolerable and should not exist, but the students were prepared to do what they could to alleviate suffering in spite of the risks involved. In addition to the dangers of infection with tuberculosis, typhoid and lesser bacteria there was ever present violent crime and almost no visible police presence in most of the black townships.

In addition to the efforts of charities, students and those who chose to serve in black hospitals, schools and missionary stations, many other whites made positive contributions. Churches and undemonstrative groups of housewives and men's clubs set up feeding schemes, endowed centres that distributed blankets and warm clothing and made sure that their own staff had decent accommodation. Some paid for small homes to be built and others for the domestic help and her children to see their private doctors or to attend good schools. All of which I witnessed at first hand.

People who behaved in an open, friendly and humane way were generally rewarded with loyalty and affection, though not always. There are several heart-warming examples that still come to mind.

When in our late teens, several of us were friendly with the son of a wealthy family which lived in the Johannesburg district. Jack Simons was a member of our university group and although not particularly athletic had access to his family's private tennis court. On one occasion, 4 of us were invited to play a few games there late in the afternoon and to stay on for a modest supper and a few beers afterwards. Jack's parents were away for a day or two and so the kitchen was supervised entirely by Stephen Bhengu, a small Zulu man who, to judge by his white hair, was about 70 years of age. At the end of the meal and when the dishes had been washed, Stephen came to find us in a room where we were drinking coffee and gossiping. Dressed in his immaculate white jacket and trousers he asked if anything else was required and, after being thanked and told we needed nothing more, made a final comment before withdrawing. What touched me particularly was that the dignified old man, standing to attention, looked around our company of unfinished and spoiled white youngsters and said "Then, very goodnight chap". The "s" was omitted.

A more famous example was provided by the friendship between a great Zulu pathfinder and Ian Player, the conservationist, philosopher and saviour of the white rhino in Southern Africa. Player was warden of the Umfolozi Game Reserve and later the founder of the Wilderness Leadership movement that was based in Natal and still operates within the Zululand game reserves. Basically he was a man who believed that re-establishing links between city men and women and nature in the raw could be more than simply life-enhancing; ultimately they might save the environment, wild animals and mankind's sanity.

At a fairly early stage in his career, Player met and worked with Magqubu Ntombela, one of the black game guards who were appointed as assistants to the white wardens in their work. Magqubu, who never mastered English, was born in 1900 to the young wife of a Zulu warrior of the Ngobamakosi regiment. His grandfather had been an *induna* or captain under the great (and bloodthirsty) Zulu king Shaka. Magqubu's father, naturally of the same stock, had been present when Chelmsford's men were defeated at Isandlwana and claimed to have killed four redcoats, possibly Welshmen from Brecon. About a century later, Magqubu visited Wales with Ian Player and went to Brecon Cathedral where the old regimental colours of the once defeated regiment hang. His purpose was to make peace with the spirits of the dead soldiers and pray for them on behalf of his father. For the first and probably the last time Zulu words of praise echoed in that place.

As a traditional umZulu, Magquba was heir to a long and vivid oral history that included talk of the old conservation practices of the Zulus. He could understand and interpret the landscape, appreciating both its practical and spiritual meaning. In 1959, Ntombela and Player, who was younger by some twenty years, began leading the first trails into the wilderness areas. Their objective was to expose people from within the country or from abroad to the spirit of the land, the tranquillity of nature and the unique magic of wilderness. Towards evening, Magqubu would go on ahead of Player and his group of pilgrims as pathfinder and to light a campfire. Later, they all sat around it, eating, enjoying a cold beer perhaps and putting the world to rights. Magqubu, who was an adept mimic, would often entertain the visitors with tales of wild beasts illustrated with his gestures and sounds. He could be relied upon to present a Zulu charade *par excellence.*

This experience had a profound impact upon visitors and support for the preservation of the wild places grew apace, as people realised there was an important connection between wilderness and urban environments. As the Magqubu Ntombela Foundation has pointed out, the prophets of all the great religions have gone into the wilderness to be alone and to find inner stillness. This is truly what has been called *the peace that the world cannot give.*

Player and Ntombela worked together for about 40 years and their legacy remains in capable hands. When he was dying, Magqubu sent for his white friend Madolo, as Player was called by the Zulus. In the beautiful and fitting obituary he wrote for this great man, Ian Player described how he sat in tears beside his friend and teacher and how the women of the Shembe church sang outside the door of Magqubu's simple hut, easing the old man's journey into paradise. Player was sure that when his own call came he would be guided across the divide by the bright light of a campfire. His Zulu friend would be sitting there, waiting for him.

There is another true story that might help to remind us of how goodwill between black and white has been wasted by greedy fools, liberal fanatics and narrow-minded idiots, both white and black. It concerns a black man, named Lucas Majozi, and the battle of El Alamein.

The South African armed forces involved in World War ll were largely made up of white and coloured soldiers with a number of black men employed as non-combatants. Members of The Native Military Corps could not carry firearms but served in other roles, that of stretcher-bearer being the most dangerous.

During the Battle of El Alamein, the South African brigades became trapped and pinned down by enemy fire in a minefield. Casualties were very high and stretcher-bearers worked in the midst of the crossfire tending to the wounded and carrying them from the battlefield. One of these brave men, who rescued many of his white countrymen, was Lucas Majozi. Under heavy machine-gun fire, severely wounded himself, Majozi returned to the slaughter time after time to do his duty. When told to have his wounds dressed, he refused and went back to the battlefield. After his partner became a casualty and could no longer bear one end of the stretcher, Majozi went out again and again to carry wounded soldiers in on his back. In the end, he collapsed from exhaustion and loss of blood.

Lucas Majozi was awarded the Distinguished Conduct Medal for his efforts. At the time the much revered South African General, Dan Pienaar, had this to say:

This soldier did most magnificent and brave things. With a number of bullets in his body he returned time after time into a veritable hell of machine gun fire to pull out wounded men. He is a man of whom South Africa can well be proud. He is a credit to this country.

He survived to go home and become a police sergeant and died at the age of only 53. What a legacy; what an example of self-sacrifice. Had Majozi been a white man from Potter's Bar and had there been a less racist, pedantic and petty commander of the 8th Army than the narcissistic little Unionist Bernard Montgomery, he must surely have been awarded the Victoria Cross. It is utterly shameful that this was not the case.

Two other members of the Native Military Corps, Job Maseko and Berry Gazi received the Military Medal for bravery in the field. Both risked their lives on behalf of their (mostly white) comrades and both died penniless and forgotten, to the thorough disgrace of both white South Africa and the British Empire. If the actions of these black men did not demonstrate love of neighbour, affection for the young white soldiers, and obedience both to the warrior traditions of their own race and to the commandments they must have learnt at mission school then I am at a loss for words.

One could write a very long book detailing the humane behaviour of whites and blacks towards one another in South Africa but it would lost upon half-baked students, the newly rampant black racialists of BLM and their many dim-witted, deluded, psychoneurotic supporters in England and America.

BROOKHOUSE

Most settled, well-balanced, men of mature years are content to lead their lives in quiet obscurity, troubling few and going their way without attracting much notice. Long ago, just such a man kept a shop in a place called Westville, close to the rooms where I worked as the junior partner in an established general practice.

The dilapidated building that housed Brookhouse Engineering had probably once been a service station or perhaps an outlet for the sales of second-hand cars. The shop was on a feeder road, no more than 20 paces from what was then a new 4-lane highway that extended from Durban, on the Natal coast, to Pietermaritzburg some 55 miles further inland. The front room of the building had been altered in a rather casual and untidy manner to make space for a low wooden counter behind which Mr Brookhouse held court. He was a gnarled, skinny fellow of perhaps 65 with a very blunt and dismissive way of communicating both with his customers and with his staff. From some ore-mining town in northern England he spoke in the curious (to most people) unmusical accent of that area. He mastered neither Afrikaans nor Zulu and so, in the manner of many Anglophones, would simply raise his voice when he wished to be heard by people from those backgrounds. Of course this technique never really worked and it was fortunate that most of his transactions with customers were very simple.

Mr Brookhouse's shop was essentially a small hardware store and the back room was awash with screws, nails, paint and all the other goods usually found in such places. His preoccupation, and indeed *forte*, was not sales but the mending electrical appliances, notably kettles, irons and stoves. When these were brought to him, he would invariably examine them closely, note that they were American, German or even Japanese and then, adopting a stern tone of voice, pronounce that they were "bloody foreign rubbish"; the key words pronounced "bloodie" and "roobish". He was never known to describe anything British in that way, possibly quite reasonably given that his heyday was all of 60 years ago and his home country had yet to self-destruct. In any event, he was a fine workman and almost any appliance would be returned to its owner as good as new, together with the unsolicited advice never to waste money on "bloody foreign rubbish" again.

One suspects that Brookhouse was also biased against any Sunday dinner other than roast beef and Yorkshire pudding. Sadly, it is unlikely that he ever sampled a marvellous *bryani*, superb curried chicken or vegetable *samosa* in all the many years he spent in Natal amongst its large and talented Indian population. Whether he ever attended a South African *braaivleis* (barbecue) with its burned meat of every kind and ice-cold lager is unknown.

Brookhouse liked to keep watch in the front of his shop and there he stayed most of the day, he behind the counter and one or more lazy-looking, brown tabby-cats sitting in the sun at the window. The store-room, a space at the back of the shop, was his wife Elsie's domain and she spent her time there, if not hiding from Brookhouse himself then presumably stock-taking or perhaps just drinking tea (English Breakfast variety; one shilling and ten pence per packet from Handy Green Grocers). Whenever a customer wanted anything from the store-room, Brookhouse would look over the top of his spectacles and shout orders to his long-suffering wife. On a command such as, "Elsie, bring a dozen one inch brass screws for Mr Cameron", she would appear looking flustered and slightly downcast, hand him a small paper-packet containing the screws and immediately retreat to her post in the back of the shop. Possibly she would rather have been in Warrington or Blackpool drinking tea or playing Bingo with her friends, all of them stylish in opaque stockings and curlers beneath scarves or hairnets.

Mrs Brookhouse was protective of the only other member of staff, a young rural Zulu named Simon, who had only a limited grasp of the plain, South African, English he had been taught during 4 years of schooling provided by a mission station in the Valley of a Thousand Hills. She would patiently explain any if not all of the incomprehensible instructions that were issued to him from time to time by Brookhouse himself. Providing Simon, whose real name was Sipho, with a simple translation of what had been said by the boss in his strange northern accent was, of course, no mean achievement.

Not every story has a happy ending, alas! The undistinguished, blunt, insignificant, little, Mr Brookhouse, as so often with Britons of his stripe, came to meet his death heroically. The highway in front of his shop was built with two traffic lanes running in each direction, two east and two west, with a grass-covered division, about three paces wide, in the middle. Traffic was not all that heavy by modern standards but cars came by every 15 or 20 seconds in both directions and at speed. One afternoon, when the shop was quiet, the perennially grumpy Mr Brookhouse noticed that one of his beloved tabby-cats, Henry, was missing. It seems the cat had chased after a cheeky sparrow that had come to the front of the shop. Henry had crossed the road and was stranded in the middle of the freeway, walking back and forth on the grass division, mewing pitifully between 4 lanes of speeding cars. No animal-lover would be surprised to learn that the forthright, flinty, but clearly soft-hearted old man never considered the danger involved and went out onto the freeway to rescue his beloved friend. One might say that was a very brave and typically foolish English thing to do.

Poor decent, noble, reckless, Mr Brookhouse, God bless him. A speeding car, driven by the inevitable testosterone-fuelled moron, hit him as he bent down to take the frightened little tabby in his arms and they died instantly; together. In a strange way, this was not just the final moment of his life but also the finest.

Selfless acts of bravery win men medals in wartime. There were no posthumous awards for the heroic little Mr Brookhouse. Perhaps the

Saint of Assisi put in a good word for this poor soul at the gates of Heaven for there is no chance that Saint Peter would have understood his north-country accent. Take this as a reminder you chaps!

WHITE KNIGHTS

The late Mr. Brookhouse was an imperfect man, as we generally are. There were other older men who crossed my path and were no doubt flawed too but might well be considered saints by those for whom they cared.

Several come to mind from amongst many exemplary characters of my father's generation. Their efforts were ignored or went largely unrecognised by that same deranged segment of society that still spends more time signalling its own virtue than actually putting a shoulder to the wheel and working to improve the lot of others.

Prime examples were the substantial number of older men (and women) who were actively involved in founding, financing and developing African Feeding Schemes, the Cape Flats Distress Association and the Valley Trust, amongst other organisations. The Valley Trust story is particularly instructive.

In about 1950 a young doctor named Halley Stott made what might now seem like an obvious observation. He noticed that many of his Zulu patients would come to hospital suffering from diseases that were preventable and were quite often related to poor nutrition. They would be treated fairly successfully and go home, only to return again a few months later, once again "running on empty". Clearly their basic diet and way of life needed corrective attention.

Stott bought land in the Valley of 1000 Hills Reserve, an inland area some 30 miles from Durban, and built a clinic there. He employed African nurses to advise patients on diet and to make follow-up home visits. Later, activities expanded to include instruction in agricultural techniques that were suitable for local soil and climatic conditions. Simple farming methods were taught to people whose traditions were once those of hunter-gatherers, and a spirit of cooperation and self-help was fostered. Sources of clean water were identified and captured and poor families given small flocks of chickens, seed, natural fertiliser, fencing and the moral support they needed to succeed. Mothers who brought sick children to the clinic were taught simple rules of preventative medicine, such as the safe use of water and sewage disposal, by trained Zulu assistants who were able to instruct them in the vernacular. The expansion of all this work led to the formation of The Valley Trust as a non-profit organisation.

For the first few decades of its existence, the Trust was administered and financed almost entirely by white philanthropists. The success of the endeavour was such that the Trust became well known and students and older individuals eager to find answers to the problems of rural Africa visited in droves. The principles learnt were applied with success elsewhere in many deprived communities.

After eighty years the Valley Trust still stands as a monument to human decency and as a reproach to certain of the white political classes who viewed it with some suspicion in the apartheid years. Many of their black successors today are no better and seem disinterested and motivated not so much by compassion for the poor as by the accrual, largely through corruption, of personal wealth and power. The Trust has a fully multiracial board, headed as I write by S'bongiseni Vilakazi, and remains true to its original strategic objectives.

The objectives are:

To improve the knowledge of health and healthy practices in the rural community.

To facilitate access to resources that promote healthy and productive living.

To strengthen the resilience of households.

To stimulate the participation of community members in the local and broader economies and ensure the sustainability of the Trust in future.

By all accounts the Valley Trust is living up to those values.

Halley Stott continued to take an interest in the expansion of the work that he began more than 50 years earlier until shortly before his death. What a legacy for one modest, unheralded and unsung, white South African to leave behind! A very clear example of a man who put hedonism to one side and did his best to follow the second great commandment of Jesus Christ:

Thou shalt love thy neighbour as thyself.

Oscar Wollheim was another such compassionate man. In his time, he did great things actively and at personal cost to alleviate the sufferings of the coloured ("mixed-race") people living in poverty and misery near Cape Town. He is yet another example of a great man who is almost certainly unheard of amongst the fashionable and largely useless liberal theorists who poison the collective mind of the current generation.

By all means let us find amusement in silly, immodest and passing diversions but, at the same time, never forget the humanity and quiet decency of good men like Stott, Wollheim and Brookhouse. They and many others have passed by largely unseen and unrecognised by the herd and, more often than not, have no memorial.

Considering their contributions to South African society brings lines from a mystical English poem by Walter de la Mare to mind:

**TELL THEM THAT I CAME AND NO ONE ANSWERED,
THAT I KEPT MY WORD.**

ABOUT THE AUTHOR

The author is a retired physician, medical researcher and university professor who has turned to horticulture and writing as distractions from the world outside and for the amusement of himself and others.

He was born in South Africa where he attended high school in Cape Town and university in Johannesburg where he qualified as a medical doctor and enjoyed success as a track athlete. He later completed a degree (M.Sc.) in exercise physiology, graduated D.Phil. at Oxford University, earned a D.Sc. at his *alma mater* and became a Fellow of the colleges of physicians of South Africa, London and Ireland. He worked internationally as a clinical pharmacologist, most notably with the late Dr. Ariel Reyes in Montevideo, and spent much of his time at home teaching medical students and attending to black patients in what is now Kwa-Zulu Natal. He moved to Ireland permanently in 1991 where he continued to teach and do practical research until retiring in 2005. He has had a home near Lismore, County Waterford since 1988 and still lives there.